Praise for *The Christian Mama's Guide to Parenting*

Working with parents of toddlers, the question they want answered is: "Am I doing okay as a parent?" In Erin's book, moms and dads will get the reassurance they are looking for during this challenging phase of parenting. Moms will not only laugh, but love the confidence that they'll feel as they learn to build their kids up mentally and spiritually in these fun and formative years.

—KATHI LIPP, SPEAKER AND AUTHOR OF
21 WAYS TO CONNECT WITH YOUR KIDS

A must-have guide for frazzled moms everywhere. With the perfect blend of practical advice, spiritual insight, and humor, Erin MacPherson assures us we're not alone and gives us the tools to raise our toddlers God's way.

—SARAH FORGRAVE, INSPIRATIONAL
AUTHOR AND MOTHER OF A TWO-YEAR-OLD

Wish you had a mentor to help you through those toddler years? Well, now you do! Erin shares a witty, wild, and wonderful guide for tackling those not-so-terrible twos! Addressing it all—from discipline to potty training to tantrums to education to getting your kid to eat and sleep and so much more, Erin helps parents keep things in God's perspective. She even provides a daddy-to-daddy guide to help him on the journey. Get in the groove and go for the gold!

—SUSAN MATHIS, BEST-SELLING AUTHOR AND
FOUNDING EDITOR OF *THRIVING FAMILY* MAGAZINE

Erin MacPherson has written a parenting book that is engaging, delightful and humorous and most importantly, offers excellent insight in helping parents enrich their children spiritually in a very relatable way.

, PEDIATRIC ER NURSE
OF *PROOF* AND *POISON*

As a mom of two boys, now in college, and an early childhood educator for the past fifteen years, I've seen practically every toddler behavior and read many ways to handle those behaviors. *The Christian Mama's Guide to Parenting a Toddler* is a laugh-out-loud, heart-stirring approach to shaping and empowering your toddler into the person Jesus created him to be. Erin's real-life stories and approaches show parenting isn't easy, but with her practical advice parents can leave the toddler years without losing their sanity. If we are teaching our children how to be like Jesus, we need to model it in our homes from the time our children bless us with their presence.

—LISA JORDAN, EARLY CHILDHOOD
EDUCATOR AND AWARD-WINNING AUTHOR OF
LAKESIDE REUNION AND *LAKESIDE FAMILY*

Reading *The Christian Mama's Guide to Parenting a Toddler* is like getting to peer in through the windows of another mom's home. A huge sigh of relief; she's not perfectly put together and neither are her kids. With a sense of humor, expert advice, and a solid faith, though, this mother of three has figured out quite a few savvy ways to make these years mostly enjoyable and not so "terrible."

—RACHEL RANDOLPH, COAUTHOR
OF *WE LAUGH, WE CRY, WE COOK*

Erin MacPherson is the best friend you've always wanted—witty, wise, informative, and godly. In her Christian Mama's Guide series, she gives practical insight and suggestions laced with biblical teaching and sound advice. As the mother of four (2, 4, 27, and 28 year olds) and the grandmother of six, I found her series to be refreshing, encouraging, and applicable. This is a must-read series for new parents—encouraging, empowering, and equipping you in Christ to set your child up for success.

—LESLIE MONTGOMERY, AUTHOR OF *A
PARENT'S GUIDE TO SPIRITUAL WARFARE*

Erin MacPherson has a way of giving good, sound advice in the same way a mother might sneak a healthy dose of vitamins into a spoonful of ice cream. I chuckled my way through her pages until, by the end, I realized I'd received life-saving wisdom from above, through a friend walking alongside me.

—FAITH BOGDAN, AUTHOR OF *WHO
ARE ALL THESE CHILDREN AND WHY
ARE THEY CALLING ME MOM?*

THE
CHRISTIAN MAMA'S GUIDE

TO PARENTING A TODDLER

Other Books by Erin MacPherson

The Christian Mama's Guide to Having a Baby
The Christian Mama's Guide to Baby's First Year
The Christian Mama's Guide to the Grade School Years

THE
CHRISTIAN MAMA'S GUIDE

TO PARENTING A TODDLER

———

Everything You

Need to Know to

Survive (*and Love*)

Your Child's Terrible Twos

———

ERIN MACPHERSON

THOMAS NELSON
Since 1798

NASHVILLE   DALLAS   MEXICO CITY   RIO DE JANEIRO

Published in Nashville, Tennessee, by Thomas Nelson. Thomas Nelson is a registered trademark of Thomas Nelson, Inc.

Thomas Nelson, Inc., titles may be purchased in bulk for educational, business, fund-raising, or sales promotional use. For information, please e-mail SpecialMarkets@ ThomasNelson.com.

Scripture quotations are taken from The Holy Bible, New International Version®, NIV ®. Copyright © 1973, 1978, 1984, 2011 by Biblica, Inc.™Used by permission of Zondervan. All rights reserved worldwide. www.zondervan.com

Library of Congress Control Number: 2013930850

ISBN: 9780849964756

Printed in the United States of America

13 14 15 16 17 RRD 6 5 4 3 2 1

*To my absolutely precious (and hardly
ever terrible) nieces and nephews:
Jacob Hoffman
Jude Schuknecht
Hadassah Dusan
Caden Pierce
Greta Schuknecht
Emberly Pierce
Asa Dusan
Holden Hoffman
Elsie Schuknecht
Alma Dusan*

Contents

Acknowledgments

Soli *Deo Gloria.* To God alone be the glory. That's my prayer for this book. I am acutely aware of the fact that every good gift comes from the Lord, and I am eternally grateful for everything He has given me—I am so blessed.

I know the cover of this book says, "Terrible Twos"—and trust me: I've dealt with my share of "terrible two" moments—but I am so blessed to be mom to three beautiful children who make me laugh and smile, and who fill my days with enough stories to keep my writing interesting. So thank you to my kids, Joey, Kate, and Will, who have made my journey as a mom worth every moment.

Huge enormous and heartfelt thanks to my sister, Alisa, who pored over these chapters with a fine-tooth comb, sharing her ideas and thoughts to make every page better. I can't write a sentence—much less a book—without your help. Thank you. And to my dad, who happily read and reread every word, telling me how I could adjust words and ideas to make the book flow. And to my mom—who gives the best discipline and parenting advice ever, thank you for sharing your expertise, your ideas, your thoughts, your notes, and your insights. And thanks to Cameron, who happily watched the kids (over and over and over) so I could write, and to Troy, who, besides my dad, is probably my biggest cheerleader in my writing. (That said, I promise to never call either of you "cheerleaders" ever again.)

To the women at my MOPS table who have seen me in my worst toddler-mommy moments and still like me enough to sit with me at a table every week. I'm not sure I could survive those long "unhappy" hours without the wonderful and supportive women who stand by me through thick and thin: my cousin Angie Ekse, Anna Martin, Barbara Jones, Hildi Nicksic, Jessica Miller, Joanne Kraft, Kathi Lipp, Laura Marion-Faul, Michelle Halvorsen, Rachel Spies, Rebecca Palmer, Sarah Jordan, Sharmon Coleman, Shellie Deringer, and Stevi Schuknecht. Thank you for sweet text messages, kind words, afternoon visits, playdates, and reminders that God is ultimately in control—not me.

I also thank my amazing work team at WeAreTeachers—Donnine Souhrada, Jennifer Prescott, Hannah Hudson, and Cami Eastman, to name a few—who went out of their way to support me as I wrote this book. I love working with you and am so blessed to be part of such an amazing and creative team.

As always, thank you to the people who helped me with their professional insights as I wrote—especially Jordyn Redwood, Jeremy Gabrysch, Amy Allert, Kathi Lipp, and Alisa Dusan and to my brilliant team—both my agent Rachelle Gardner and my Thomas Nelson editing team, Debbie, Adria, Kate, and Lori. Y'all are truly incredible.

Introduction

What Happened to My Sweet Baby?

Your baby is—or at least was—about as close to perfection as you'll find this side of heaven. Those dreamy grins every time you walked into the room. The sweet melody of ba-ba-la-la-las in the baby monitor as you woke up each morning. Those moments when she snuggled close and fell asleep on your shoulder. Pure, sweet almost-perfection.

But recently, have you noticed something changing? Like those dreamy grins being replaced by snarls? And that sweet melody of ba-ba-la-la-las sounding an awful lot like, "No! Mine! No! No! No!"? And those snuggle-close-and-fall-asleep moments getting fewer and farther between?

Just as you were getting that whole baby thing down pat, your kid decides to up and turn one and a half on you. And suddenly, you're afraid to go out in public because your kid might pitch a royal fit, but you don't want to stay home because your kid may have a tantrum. You can't go to restaurants (he might smoosh peas into the carpet) or to parks (he may hit someone) or to stores (he might climb the shelves). How do you survive?

I remember the day I realized that my son was in the terrible twos. We were at the park with the other moms in my MOPS group, and Will picked up a pebble (okay, it was a rock) and threw it at another kid. Gulp. After a very long (and very passionate) lecture on why rock throwing isn't a nice thing to do, I was certain Will wouldn't do it again. He was so contrite. And surely he hadn't done it on purpose. He was only *one*! So I hugged my oh-so-sweet son tightly and sent him off to play. And as soon as he escaped my grip, he smiled innocently at me, picked up another rock, and threw it at the same kid. Harder this time. Uh-oh. *Helllllo,* terrible twos.

So, what now? How do you survive when your kid can't make it through the day (okay, the minute) without throwing a massive tantrum? And what do you do when he thinks that a balanced diet should consist solely of mac & cheese and chocolate chips? And how do you discipline a kid who can't understand the difference between "steal" and "share"? And how in the world can you go grocery shopping when your kid's throwing toys out of the cart every twelve seconds as you stock up in the bulk-foods aisle?

It's time to adjust your mama game plan. You *can* be the mom of a one-and-a-half-year-old and still go into public and come home (somewhat) sane. And you can love God, love your husband, and (yes) even love your fit-throwing, no-saying, rock-throwing kid while doing it. Here's how.

*A note for my particularly scrupulous readers: you may notice that most of the pronouns in this book are male. This was a decision made by my editors and me in order to keep the copy simple and consistent. It in no way means that that this book is more applicable to boys or that I intended the tips and advice in this book to be just for boys. So, if you happen to have a daughter (like I do), please mentally substitute "her" for "him" and "she" for "he" as you read. And then write a very serious letter to whoever invented the English language, letting them know how much easier our lives would be if pronouns weren't gender specific.

ONE

Getting into the Toddler Mama Groove

Surviving and Thriving in the Toddler Years

I took my one-and-a-half-year-old niece, Greta, to McDonald's a few days ago. I'm not sure if that makes me a bad auntie (she's asked for McNuggets for breakfast, lunch, and dinner every day since) or a cool auntie (I let her get fries ... *shhhhh!*)— but regardless, she loved it. And I did too. Except for one thing: Greta—adorable, sweet and precious Greta—is smack-dab in the middle of the terrible twos.

We walked into the play area, and before I could set my tray on a table, Greta ran up to another kid who was putting on his shoes and shouted, "No! Mine!" Turns out Greta was under the impression that everything in the room belonged to her. The slide? Mine! The giant piano on the wall? Mine! The little baby that another woman was putting in a high chair? You guessed it. Mine! It was hilarious. And aside from having to remind Greta 15,324 times to be sweet, we had a wonderful time.

I told my sister-in-law the story, and she wasn't quite as amused. You see, Greta's plunge from delectable baby to delectable-yet-exasperating toddler happened very quickly and very unexpectedly. One day, Greta was her normal, sweet self—singing sleepily in her crib, eating whatever delicacy her mama put on her plate, and playing nicely with her cousins. The next day, Greta woke up a different kid. She whined. She said no. She threw her veggies on the floor. And she screamed, "Mine!" at anyone and everyone who dared come within fifteen feet of one of her toys.

My sister-in-law is beyond frustrated—and rightfully so. I remember feeling the same way when my kids hit the terrible twos. Suddenly, all my parenting skills were tested. All the rules were changed. And all my lovely walk-in-the-park moments were ruined by massive temper tantrums and whining fits. I realized I had to get my mama groove back because my sweet baby was no longer a sweet baby, and if we were being honest, I was no longer a sweet-baby mama. I was a frustrated mama. And an annoyed mama. And the kind of mama who spent more time saying no to my kid than he spent saying no to everyone else. Which was a lot.

Being the parent of a one-and-a-half-year-old is overwhelming. Remember back in your new-mama days when the mere thought of feeding and bathing and diapering a baby seemed overwhelming? Remember that? Well, now you're an old pro. Being a toddler mama is a lot like that; it feels impossible at first. It seems you'll never be able to go to the mall—or church—again. But you'll figure it out. And before long you'll be able to handle a whiny meltdown while calmly filing your nails and sipping an espresso.

How to Get into the Toddler Mama Groove

1. Give yourself a break.

I'm a perfectionist, so I tend to think of my kids' behavior as a direct reflection on me. And then, when my kid acts obnoxiously, I blame myself for being a terrible mother. But mama mantra #1345 begs to differ: You are not a terrible mother because your kid just smeared Desitin all over your mother-in-law's antique quilt. Or hasn't eaten anything besides peanut butter and Cheerios in nine days. Or just stole a toy from another kid at playgroup.

I'm not saying you shouldn't deal with these issues—you should—but simply that you can't be hard on yourself because your kid is having a bad day. Motherhood is hard, and no mom in the history of the entire world has been a perfect mama—no one. With that in mind, even in your worst mama moments, cut yourself some slack. God has used some of the hardest times I've had as a mom—times when I wasn't sure if I would survive the day, much less eighteen years—to show me how to depend on Him. And in order for God to use these trials to help me learn and grow, I have to let go of them and give them to God. Only He can make our paths—and our children's paths—straight.

2. Give yourself a time-out from your kid.

Sometimes you just need a time-out. I remember a day like that. My son Joey had thrown a huge fit in Target because I hadn't bought him a chocolate milk (mean mommy, right?), and that had escalated to a hysterically whiny car ride and a full-on toy-throwing tantrum when we got home. I called my mom. She told me to bring him over to her house.

I vegged in front of the TV while she took him to play in the sandbox and read him books. He calmed down. I calmed down. And by the time I had to go home to make dinner, I was a different mama—calm, cool, collected, and totally in love with my adorable son. Whoever said that absence makes the heart grow fonder was almost certainly the mom of a one-and-a-half-year-old. I can be at my wit's end, but after just an hour away, be rushing home for a chubby-armed toddler hug.

So, on those can't-get-through-five-minutes-without-an-issue days, don't be afraid to call a friend, call your mother, call *someone*. No one can do it alone, and chances are that your mother or your sister or your best girlfriend would be happy to take your kid to McDonald's for an hour or two . . . and return them full of chicken nuggets and French fries.

3. Plan Your Days to Include Movement.

In the past, you may have been able to get by with lazing around all morning and spending the afternoon reading stories, but most toddlers are active and need a lot of activity. And by "need a lot of activity," I mean that if you don't make sure your kid runs around for at least two hours out of every day, you're pretty much guaranteed a five-star meltdown at nap time and an eight-star fit at dinner.

So, for your sanity (and your kid's), try to work some activity into every day. One of my favorite things to do with my kids is to go into the backyard and play soccer. They love it because it's fun. I love it because it counts as exercise for them *and* for me—and because a couple of years ago, after a couple of weeks of backyard soccer practice, my husband commented on my "sexy soccer-player calves." Let's just say I became a regular soccer fiend after that. Even a quick walk to the park or around the neighborhood can burn some of that pent-up toddler energy, especially if you let your kid walk at her pace instead of yours. Of course, that means you won't get anywhere quickly, but who cares? At least you'll be able to inspect every single acorn you see along the way.

4. Pray. For Yourself.

I know you're praying for your kid. Like, all the time. But what about for yourself? It's hard to be a good mama—especially when your kid isn't exactly full of sugar and spice and everything nice. So pray for patience. Pray for wisdom. And pray that you'll be able to reflect Christ's love in your life even when you're on your last nerve.

Time-Out for Mom

For When You're Praying for Yourself as a Mother

"You have searched me, LORD,
　　and you know me.
You know when I sit and when I rise;
　　you perceive my thoughts from afar.
You discern my going out and my lying down;
　　you are familiar with all my ways.
Before a word is on my tongue
　　you, LORD, know it completely.
You hem me in behind and before,
　　and you lay your hand upon me.
Such knowledge is too wonderful for me,
　　too lofty for me to attain." (Psalm 139:1–6)

Lord God, it is such an incredible thing that you—the creator of heaven and earth—know me personally. You know my every flaw, my every strength, my every thought, and my every desire. And so, I don't have to tell You that I desperately love my children and want to do whatever it takes to raise them in a way that's pleasing to You. Lord, I need Your help. I cannot do it alone. My human ways are weak—I grow impatient and selfish and angry. But You are so much bigger than that, and I pray that You will fill me with Your Spirit so that I, in turn, can be like You. Amen.

Toddler Dictionary

Just to get you started off right on your toddler-mama journey, here's a dictionary of common toddler words.

Bedtime [bed-tahym] 1. The moment when—no matter how exhausted I've been all day—I suddenly feel wide-awake. 2. The moment when—no matter how much milk I left in my sippy cup at dinnertime—I suddenly feel extremely thirsty. 3. The moment when—no matter how independent I've felt all day—I suddenly feel extremely needy.

Binky [bing-k-*ee*] (also known as: *wubby, wubbalove, paci, pacifier*) 1. The thing that—no matter how much my mom tries—I will refuse to go to bed without. 2. The thing that—no matter how much mom tries—I will refuse to leave the house without.

Broccoli [brok-*uh*-lee] A green, treelike substance that should be immediately fed to the dog if placed on your high chair tray.

Chocolate Milk [chaw-kuh-lit milk] The only thing that will keep me from tossing a carton of eggs on the floor at the grocery store.

Crayon [krey-on] 1. The thing mom always puts in my hand when she wants me to be quiet at restaurants. 2. A tool for decorating walls, floors, and mom's super-expensive antique coffee table. 3. A yummy snack.

Dog [dawg] 1. The big thing lying on the floor that wants you to pull its tail. 2. Synonymous with "pony."

Hair [hair] A convenient place to wipe your hands after you've eaten mashed sweet potatoes or anything with maple syrup.

Mine [mahyn] 1. Something that belongs to me. 2. Something that I want to belong to me. 3. Something that once belonged to me. 4. Something that I've seen before.

Park [pahrk] 1. The place where I can run and scream as loud as I want and mom won't tell me to stop. 2. The place where I will find unlimited amounts of gravel, rocks, and dirt to roll in, get in my shoe, eat, and throw at other kids.

The Wiggles [th-uu wig-*uh*ls] 1. The absolutely hilarious guys that mom—against her best judgment—introduced me to on that day she was trying to answer sixty-two e-mails in one afternoon. 2. The fun concert that mom will—against her best judgment—take me to when they come to town. 3. The fun CD that mom will—against her best judgment—buy. 4. The fun CD that mom will—against her best judgment—play in the car CD player if I whine long enough.

Whine [wahyn] 1. The noise you make when you really, really want something. 2. The noise you make when you really, really want something and mom says no. 3. The noise you make when you really, really want something and mom still keeps saying no. 4. The noise you make when you don't remember what you wanted, but you know Mom will probably say no anyway.

Vegetable [vej-*tuh*-*buhl*] A fun toy that mom puts on your dinner plate so you have something to throw during dinnertime.

Your Toddler is Fabulous (Even If She's Fabulously Obnoxious at Times)

Even in the middle of the most hysterical, most obnoxious, most terrible one-and-a-half fit, if you look really, really close, your kid will still be pretty darn cute. That's because your kid is a fabulously amazing (and independent) creation of God, and even in the middle of her one-and-a-half-year-old glory, she is still pretty darn amazing.

The thing about the terrible twos is that they really aren't that terrible. Sure, your kid acts terrible from time to time, but it's because she is growing and learning and trying to figure out the world. And sometimes that figuring manifests itself as whining. And sometimes that growing manifests itself as fit-throwing. But in the middle of it all, God is working in your kid's life, and you get the incredible privilege of getting a front-row seat to it all.

It's easy to get frustrated with one-and-a-half-year-olds, but it's also easy to love them for the real, honest, and utterly adorable children of God that they are. And with that in mind, let's get on with our loving—and surviving—of the toddler years.

TWO

Heart, Mind, and Soul

Getting a Handle on Toddler Discipline

Your kid needs Jesus.

Yes, he probably needs a snack and a nap and a good old-fashioned lecture on the importance of manners, but most of all, your kid needs Jesus. And no matter how many tantrums your kid throws or how many toys he flat-out refuses to share, toddler discipline all boils down to one thing: your kid needs Jesus. To grow his heart. To shape his mind. And to soothe his soul.

As a mom, I tend to get caught in the trap of thinking my kids need *me*. They need a mom who keeps a flowchart of discipline strategies on her fridge and knows exactly when to Love-and-Logic them and when to send them to time-out. A mom who can keep her cool in the midst of the biggest terrible-two meltdown. A mom who is willing to go the distance to make sure her kids behave. And while all those things are important, thank God that He is there behind the scenes, working to capture my kids' hearts, minds, and souls. Because standing on my own strength, I'm an utter failure when it comes to discipline.

Like most things when it comes to parenting toddlers, this was something I learned the hard way when my two-year-old threw himself into an upstairs window during nap time. Yeah, that's right. Joey took a running start and plowed headfirst into the upstairs, low-hanging window because he didn't want to nap. That kind of makes you feel better about your kid's behavior *and* your parenting, doesn't it?

Fortunately, Joey was just fine. He hit it hard enough to spiderweb the glass, which cost $250 to replace—*thankyouverymuch,* strong-willed toddler—but he was uninjured. He didn't get cut or bruised or go flying out the window and onto the hard concrete below. I, however, was not just fine. I was mortified. And frustrated. And really upset about the fact that I didn't have the discipline savvy to keep my precious little boy safe and sound on my watch. And after going downstairs and downing an entire bag of Ghirardelli chocolate (I'm exaggerating; a half bag was totally sufficient), I called my mom in tears. And you know what she told me? Not that I had failed as a parent. Or that Joey was a delinquent who needed to be sent to time-out until he was fourteen. She told me that he needed Jesus. That's it. My son needed Jesus.

That afternoon, sitting on the floor in my son's room, I hit my rock-bottom place when it came to discipline and parenting. I felt desperate because nothing I had done on my own strength was working. I had read all the books, all the spank-versus-time-out debates, and all the don't-let-your-kid-win-a-power-struggle strategies. And none of them seemed to be working with my son. Because what my son ultimately needed more than all those strategies is the same thing I need, for Jesus to change my heart.

Now that I've boiled toddler discipline down to simply your kid needing Jesus, I need to tell you that this doesn't mean you should just ignore discipline altogether. Because even though your kid needs Jesus, your kid also needs a parent to lead him to Jesus. And part of leading your toddler to Jesus involves sprinkling every conversation, every tender moment, and every mortifying tantrum or all-out meltdown into an opportunity to show your toddler about Jesus' perfect, holy, and saving love.

I'm Just a Mom

I'm not even going to begin to claim to be qualified to teach you about the psychology behind biblical discipline. I'm not a counselor or a behavior therapist or a teacher or a Dugger. I'm just a mom. A mom who has dealt with approximately 1,234,237 toddler fits, 234,345 whiny tantrums, and 143 I'm-not-sure-I-can-do-this-for-another-minute meltdowns (by me, not my kids). I've read the books. I've listened to the advice. I've tried. I've failed. I've tried again. And while I in no way can call myself a toddler discipline expert, I can tell you that I have been in your shoes.

In this chapter, you're not going to find the ultimate toddler discipline strategy that's guaranteed to turn your tantrum-throwing toddler into an angelic little schnookums overnight or you get your money back. I'm not going to give you a seventeen-step plan to getting your kids to behave or a list of definitive instructions on how to teach your kids about the Ten Commandments. Because those strategies don't exist. And even if they did, I'm not afraid to admit that I don't have all the answers. But I do know one thing: your kid needs Jesus.

. . . .

Time-Out for Mom

For When You're Praying for Your Kid's Heart, Soul, and Mind

"Praise the LORD. Blessed are those who fear the LORD, who find great delight in his commands. Their children will be mighty in the land; the generation of the upright will be blessed." (Psalm 112:1–2)

Lord God, I pray for my children right now. I pray that they grow up to find great delight in You so they not only fear You, but that they also love you with every inch of their being. O God, help me to guide them in that way. Give me the insight and the patience to raise them in a way that shows them Your love even from a young age. Amen.

Justice, Mercy, and Grace

I'm sure if you've been a mom for more than, say, five minutes, you've heard loads of parenting advice. People love to advise parents. Older women will corner you in the grocery store and regale you with the things they learned when their kids were kids. People on the street will tell you their tips on how to educate your child. Heck, I once had a thirteen-year-old volunteer at vacation Bible school pull me aside and give me her advice on how to help my daughter have a smooth drop-off. But after seven years of parenting and loads of parenting advice from both experts and nonexperts, I can tell you that there is one piece of parenting advice that has resonated with me more than any other. And it is to treat your kids with the same sense of justice, mercy, and grace that Christ shows us.

My mom-savvy and brilliant friend Amy Allert actually gave me this idea. She explained that, so often, we as parents focus on black-and-white discipline with our kids by giving them consequences to (hopefully) teach them to quell some misbehavior. This is important. But Amy pointed out that Jesus doesn't always give us what we deserve. He gives us what we need. And if we're going to teach our kids about Jesus, we need to go beyond simple crime-and-punishment discipline and give our kids the tools they need to turn their hearts toward Christ. This takes some mom smarts—as well as some prayer and biblical insight—but in the end, it's a way to give our kids what they need. And that's—you guessed it—Jesus.

Now, before I go any further, I need to explain what I mean by all this justice, mercy, and grace talk. To put it really simply, if your kid does something wrong, you have the choice to respond to his behavior with justice, mercy, or grace. Each of these responses teaches him something about Jesus and His infinite wisdom and love. I've found that by responding to my kids in a variety of ways, depending on each individual situation, I've opened up the doors to many meaningful conversations with my kids. I've also found that by starting out these conversations when my kids are young—too young to fully grasp Christ's love—it lays the foundation for future understanding.

Anyway, when I respond to my kids' misbehavior with justice, I give them what they deserve by giving them a logical consequence. Jesus responds to all of us with justice sometimes; He teaches us to be obedient through natural consequences. So when your kid is throwing his toys across the room, it makes sense to confiscate those toys. Or when your kid is melting down on the living room floor, it makes sense to remove him from the room to a time-out spot where he can calm down. Justice served.

But Jesus doesn't only respond to us with justice. If He did, we'd all be walking around in a perpetual state of time-out. There are times He responds to us with mercy. He mercifully lets us make unwise decisions and then forgives us even when forgiveness is undeserved. He allows us back into His presence even when He should shun us forever. And, to fully demonstrate Jesus' wisdom to our kids, there are times when we can (and should) respond to our kids in the same way. So, next time your kid decides to, say, throw a hard wooden block at your head, go pick him up and say something like, "Wow! That wasn't nice. But I know you really didn't mean to hurt me, so I'm going to forgive you. Can we build a tower together?" Mercy given.

There's one more piece to this whole puzzle, and it's perhaps the most difficult one of all for us parents to grasp. God sometimes deals with us with justice, and other times He gives us mercy. But God also gave us the ultimate gift of grace. He sent His perfect and unblemished Son to die for us on the cross, giving us the totally undeserved gift of salvation. To put this in toddler terms, while we were melting down and throwing a massive tantrum on the living room floor, He fixed us a massive ice cream sundae. And then He scooped us off the floor and into our high chairs and let us dig into layers of chocolate sauce and whipped cream. Grace received.

When Amy explained this concept to me, I at first revolted. I'd be a crazy woman to give my kid ice cream when he's misbehaving. But that's not the point. The point is that we can't look at discipline as a formula, as a set of rules that block us into simple consequences and responses to our kids' behavior. Instead, we have to prayerfully consider each circumstance and respond to our kids as God would respond to us: with love, wisdom, and a strong sense of justice, mercy and grace.

Discipline That Teaches

I want to make it really (really) clear that I'm not telling you to reward your toddler's misbehavior with sugary snacks. Can you imagine what would happen if you responded with grace next time your toddler throws a fit in the grocery store? "Yes, sweetheart, I know you're on the floor, kicking the nice lady who is trying to buy milk, but let me show you some grace and buy you a box of cookies. There. That's a nice kid. Oh, let me throw in a Reese's Peanut Butter Cup since you got up so quickly."

What I am telling you to do is to prayerfully consider how you respond to your toddler's misbehavior instead of trying to trap yourself (and your kid) into a set of disciplinary rules. I'm not going to encourage or bash any of the major parenting books—I've probably read them all and have found useful bits of information in each of them—but simply want to tell you there is no perfect solution. There's no gold-carat program or perfect technique that works every time. There simply is no 1-2-3 magic potion that will teach your kids to behave.

I've found, when it comes to discipline, the claws sometimes come out. Passionate debates rage on all sides—especially when it comes to spanking. People camp out on their hills and fight to prove that their discipline method is the one and only way to parent a child. I want to insert my two cents and say that this isn't a hill to die on. Each child has been created with a unique personality and unique needs, and what works for one kid probably won't for another. So prayerfully consider your discipline strategy—read books, study, learn, and listen to advice—and then create a strategy that works best for your unique kid in your unique family. Then move forward with the end goal being to lead your kid to Jesus. Get to know your child's unique personality in the process.

With that said, when you're dealing with a toddler, you'll probably have to err on the side of justice most of the time. Two-year-olds need structure and definite consequences for their behavior. So, while you may choose to sprinkle in some mercy and grace from time to time, with toddlers, justice is king. As your kid gets older, and once you've laid a strong foundation in your kid's heart as to what is right and what is wrong, you may find yourself being able to integrate more mercy and grace. A kid has to understand what he does deserve in a certain situation before he can receive mercy and grace as the gifts that they are. But when your toddler is young, I want to encourage you to simply pray and consider how each and every situation can teach your child about Christ. And respond accordingly.

With that in mind, I worked with my mom—a veteran early childhood educator and parenting coach who spends her days coaching parents through grace-filled discipline (see www.FamilyWings.org to learn more) to come up with some creative and practical discipline ideas that work with toddlers. Since toddler behavior is pretty straightforward—a tantrum here, a fit there, a thrown toy on the left, and a refusal to share during playgroup on the right—I feel that most of these consequences relate directly to whatever toddler behaviors you may be struggling with.

Ten Creative Consequences for Toddlers

1. **Go to time-out with your kid.** Have you ever really considered what time-out does for your kid? Yes, it teaches him that misbehavior results in a consequence—in this case, removal from the family dynamic. But my mom and I think that time-out can be much more—even for a toddler who isn't quite ready to truly contemplate his actions in a meaningful way. Next time your toddler needs a time-out, try going with him. Don't make it a fun mommy-and-me time, but simply sit down and say something like, "We're going to take a little time-out to think about what just happened. Let's just sit here for a moment quietly and pray that Jesus will help us learn from this." Sit with your toddler so he is unable to get up and also is unable to play with toys, and give him some time to think quietly. Then pray out loud that God will help your kid learn to behave.

2. **Institute a tantrum corner.** Probably the best tantrum-stopper in our house has been the tantrum corner. We designated a corner of our dining room as the tantrum corner. I told my kids that I wanted them to throw tantrums there. In fact, when they were in the tantrum corner, I expected their tantrums to be loud and obnoxious. And anytime a tantrum starts, I simply carry the offending kid into the tantrum corner, set him down, and step outside of the room. Interestingly, none of my kids are motivated to keep up the fit when they don't have an audience. (Note: This actually works in grocery stores too. More about that in the next chapter, "Tantrums 401.")

3. **Add a whine chair to the mix.** Another related tool is the whine chair. Ours is in the garage, where I can shut the door

and block the noise. Whenever your toddler starts to whine, tell him he is welcome to whine as much as he wants in the whine chair. And when he's ready to stop whining, you'll be happy to talk to him. (Note, for a young whiner, a high chair pushed into a quiet room works great, as it keeps him strapped in and out of trouble. Just listen closely for the first sign of non-whining so you can pull him out!)

4. **Read a book**. I know; reading a book is hardly a punishment, so this idea tends to skew toward "grace" instead of "justice," but I'm okay with that because this idea has worked wonders with my kids—toddlers, preschoolers, and grade-schoolers alike. I keep a stockpile of "character" books on the top shelf of my bookshelf. For toddlers, I use books like *No Hitting!* by Karen Katz and the Really Woolly books by Bonnie Rickner Jensen. When you notice your toddler hitting a friend or refusing to share, you can simply pull him up on your lap, pull out a related book, and read it together. Then gently talk about why kindness is important.

5. **Do chores**. Let me make one thing clear: having your toddler help you with chores will not actually be helpful. To you, at least. But it will help your toddler learn about teamwork, respect, and helping each other. Try saying something like "Oh no! You've made a huge mess by throwing your toys. I will help you clean it up, but then you're going to have to help me sort some laundry. Can you help me find all the socks?"

6. **Give your kid a do-over**. This might be my favorite "mercy" consequence, and it works beautifully for kids of all ages with minor misbehaviors. Next time your toddler does something small but ridiculous—like pulling the dog's tail—say something like, "Oh, I know you didn't mean to do that! Let's try it again." Then, walk your child back to where he started and have him demonstrate the right behavior—in this case, gently petting the dog.

7. **Practice makes perfect**. Your toddler can never learn how to

do the right thing if he hasn't been shown. So practice! When my friend Andi's two-year-old daughter, Rachel, refused to share any of her toys when a friend came over, Andi decided to give her some practice. Andi went to Target and bought a beautiful princess doll for herself. Andi got home, unwrapped her doll and started to play with it on the floor. Rachel, of course, made a beeline for the doll and said, "Mine!" Andi quickly explained that it was *mommy's* doll and she was playing with it, but she'd be happy to share in a few minutes. Andi and Rachel practiced. Over and over, back and forth. And— wouldn't you know it—the next time a friend came over, Rachel knew exactly what she needed to do to share.

8. **Give your kid a snack**. I know I told you that giving a sugary snack to a tantruming toddler is a bad, bad idea. And I stick to that. But I will also say that when I'm hungry, I'm cranky. And when I'm cranky, I do things I wouldn't normally do. Give your toddler the same courtesy; if he is acting downright nasty, give him a healthy snack. Now, if only your mood could change so quickly with a cheese stick.

9. **Help them calm down**. Sometimes it's just hard to find calm in the midst of chaos—but you wouldn't know anything about that, would you? My friend Kate helped her toddlers calm down after a particularly stressful meltdown by handing them a "chill out jar" (aka a mason jar with colored water and glitter, glued shut) and having them shake it up and then sit quietly until the sparkles settled.

10. **Take a cue from Aibileen**. Confession: I took notes as I read *The Help*. Aibileen and the other maids are just so brilliant when it comes to child-rearing. Anyway, the "thumb in the palm" trick—the one where Aibileen got down low to speak to her charges, making eye contact and gently pressing her thumb into the kid's palm—is a brilliant parenting move that has helped deter a tantrum and resolve the peace in our house on more than one occasion.

Infusing Your Speech with Jesus

Since I'm being all nice and sharing my mom with you (you're welcome), I decided to finish off this chapter by asking her for her number-one piece of discipline advice for kids. And since I know her and have been calling her every time I need parenting advice for almost seven years now, I wasn't surprised by what she said. But you might be.

She said the most important component to discipline isn't actually the discipline. It's the conversations you have with your kid every day, every hour, every minute. Because it's through those conversations that your kid learns that he needs Jesus to change his heart, and in doing so, he will learn to have godly character and to practice things like self-control, perseverance, kindness, forgiveness, honesty, and love.

I get it: talking to a toddler about self-control is like talking to your husband about feelings. You can talk all you want, but most of what you say is going to go way (way) over his head. But that's okay. Keep talking. Because a conversation here, a tidbit there will all built up, and one day—when your toddler is no longer a toddler—it's all going to click. And he's going to say, "I get it! Jesus loves me! And I want to show Him how much I love Him with everything I say and do." (And your husband, he's going to suddenly start gushing about his deepest feelings. Or not.)

Anyway, I know I'm talking way up in the theoretical clouds here when you probably want real-life practical advice that you can implement without having to think (much). So, I've put together eight conversation starters that even a young toddler can understand to get you talking about Jesus.

Five Come-to-Jesus Conversations to Start with Your Toddler
- "Wow! Look at that pretty rainbow. I think that's God's way of telling us how much He loves us. What other ways do you think God is showing His love for us today?"

- "You know, one of the things I love most about Jesus is that He forgives me no matter what I do. I just have to ask. Would you like to pray with me and ask Jesus for forgiveness?"
- "I sometimes just sit here and think about how amazing it is that Jesus made me just the way I am. It makes me feel thankful that He gave me a healthy body and a mind to learn about Him. He even gave me a special kid like you! What do you thank Jesus for?"
- "I really want to make Jesus smile. Want to come sit by me and talk about the things we can do to show Jesus how much we love Him?"
- "I'm feeling really worn-out today, so I'm going to spend a few minutes praying that Jesus will help me through the day. Want to join me?"

It's All About Jesus

God has given you a magnificent gift—that beautiful, smart, talented, unique, and built-for-an-eternal purpose kid that's sitting over there, stacking Duplo blocks to build a tower. That, or throwing Duplo blocks at the window to see if it'll break. What a treasure! And what a responsibility to make sure that beautiful, smart, talented, and unique kid gets exactly what he needs to fulfill the purpose he was built for. It all boils down to one thing: your kid needs Jesus. Can you show him the way?

THREE

Tantrums 401

A Requisite Course on How to Handle Toddler Tantrums

Section 1: I Was a Great Parent Before I Had Kids

Hi. My name is Erin, and I will be your professor for this course. Over the next few weeks, I'll be leading you deep into the depths of the toddler mind. We'll explore chocolate-induced meltdowns and toy-induced fits and even the troublesome but common I-don't-know-why-I'm-banging-the-wall-with-my-fists-but-I-am-doing-it-anyway tantrums. Let me warn you right up front: this is not a course for the fainthearted. Toddler tantrums can destroy the confidence of even the smuggest, most adept Christian moms. In fact, I'm pretty sure the reason I was picked to lead this course isn't because of my deep understanding of the toddler mind but because of the sheer number of toddler fits I've dealt with in the last several years. It's astounding, really. But let's get back to the beginning. Back to the time when I believed I knew all the answers. Back to the days when I didn't have any kids of my own.

I actually remember the day I realized that I was undoubtedly the best parent ever. It was early 2005, and my husband and I decided to go to dinner at Red Robin. So, we hopped into our snazzy two-door Honda Civic, opened the sunroof, and cruised on over for some burgers and endless fries. Make that burgers, fries, and endless kiddie tantrums. Because I'm telling you, that place was packed with whiny, French fry–throwing, burger-crumbling toddlers. Didn't these people know that if they couldn't figure out how to make their kids behave, then they should probably stay home and have oven-fried Dino Nuggets for dinner?

One thing I knew for sure was that I was *never, ever* going to let my kids behave like that. I knew that with clear, consistent boundaries and natural, logical consequences, my kid would just hop on the good-behavior bandwagon and happily eat steamed broccoli. All aboard! And this trip to Red Robin proved it once and for all: I was a natural parent. I mean, I had absolutely no problem figuring out exactly what all those other parents of fit-throwing toddlers were doing wrong. I was so proud of myself that I went straight home and got myself pregnant.

Two years later, that smug smile was wiped off my face when my sweet little Joey—the baby who had cooed happily and enchanted me with sweet, chubby-armed hugs—threw his first toddler tantrum. Over a cell phone. I had it. He wanted it. I said no. He arched his back, screamed at the top of his lungs, and proceeded to kick, scream, yell, and moan like . . . well . . . like I would if someone took *my* phone away. It wasn't pretty. And all the tips, strategies, advice, and ideas I had carefully devised for other parents suddenly didn't work when I tried them on my own kid.

If you haven't experienced the quintessential toddler meltdown yet, your day is coming, my friend. Yes, your day is coming. You'll be hanging out at home, having a lovely time playing blocks with your toddler, and—*bam!*—the blue block won't fit next to the red block, and when he tries to squeeze it in, the green block will fall and, well, as you can imagine, the tears will be followed by passionate destruction of the block city, which will be followed by a back-arching, fist-pounding fit.

Or you'll be at Target. Let's make it the Target toy section on Christmas Eve as you try to find one last present to overnight to your long-lost cousin's nephew. And your toddler will spot a mechanical cookie monster. And naturally, he'll want to get down on the floor underneath the stampede of shoppers to play with said cookie monster. And when you say, "No, we need to get out of here before the post office closes," he'll hear something like, "No, you're never, ever going to get to play with any toy ever again." And, well, let's just say that you'll wish you had just sent your cousin's nephew a gift card.

Toddler meltdowns are mortifying. They (a) make you feel as if you're the worst parent ever, and (b) make you want to go buy your toddler a bag of jelly beans and a Lightning McQueen toy just to make him settle down and go back to being the sweet, funny, and adorable kid you know and love. But just FYI—it's actually a known fact in tantruming academic circles that giving a child what he wants when he's throwing a tantrum usually serves to cause more tantrums. Who knew? And since bribery with candy and toys won't work, I've put together some tips on what will.

. . . .

Time-Out for Mom

For When You're Trying to Survive an Emotional Meltdown
(Both Yours and Your Kid's)

"Therefore, since we have been justified through faith, we have peace with God through our Lord Jesus Christ, through whom we have gained access by faith into this grace in which we now stand.

And we boast in the hope of the glory of God. Not only so, but we also glory in our sufferings, because we know that suffering produces perseverance; perseverance, character; and character, hope. And hope does not put us to shame, because God's love has been poured out into our hearts through the Holy Spirit, who has been given to us. You see, at just the right time, when we were still powerless, Christ died for the ungodly." (Romans 5:1–6)

Lord Jesus Christ, my peace here on earth comes only from You. And I give You my heartfelt gratitude for the hope I have through you. Without Your grace, I would be lost. I pray that my tough moments— whether it's a minor toddler meltdown or a fit of utter exhaustion and frustration on my part—will lead to perseverance, character, and ultimately, hope. Thank You, Father, for Your saving grace. Amen.

Section 2: Tantrums at Home

You should actually feel happy when your kid throws a fit at home. Yes, that's right. I'm telling you how you should feel about your kid's misbehavior. And just so you know, I have my hand on my hip and a finger wagging at you while I tell you too. But really, at-home tantrums are a good thing. Here's why: when nobody (except for maybe your nosy next-door neighbor) can see your kid's fit, nobody can see how you respond to it. And that gives you space to think a bit more off your toes and even (gasp!) make tantrum-handling mistakes. It's a closed-door dress rehearsal for the real thing. See? A good thing. So wipe that aghast look off your face and start smiling, missy. I want to see you (secretly) cheering on your toddler's next at-home fit.

Since at-home meltdowns give you the chance to figure out how to best deal with tantrums, don't be afraid to test things out a little. For example, my one-and-a-half-year-old, Will, has decided he likes to claw at the dog's eyes. And while that may sound fun to Will, it's not exactly fun for the dog. Or for me, for that matter. The best part of this little scenario is that every time I let the dog outside so he can escape his tormenter, Will throws a massive fit. He stands at the back door, pointing at the dog and screaming, "Dooooooogggg!" while pounding on the glass with his fists.

Last time this happened, I decided to try a few different strategies. Would it work if I put Will outside and let the dog stay inside? Nope. Will just screamed and pounded on the outside of the door (and as a general rule, it tends to be frowned upon to lock toddlers out of your house). Would it help if I moved Will into another room to distract him from the dog? Nope. He just screamed louder. Did getting down at eye level and talking to him calm him down? Nope. He clawed at *my* eyes. Finally, I just ignored him. Let him pound his fist on the door. Let the dog gloat behind his glass wall of protection. A few minutes later, the fit stopped. Will forgot about the dog. And fortunately, the dog forgot about Will. For a few minutes, at least.

See, at-home fits are fun! You get to try out all sorts of fun things and you might even have some screeching, wailing background music to accompany the drama. And just to make sure you get maximum enjoyment out of the process, here are a few of my best at-home tantrum tips:

Ten Tricks for Fighting at-Home Tantrums

1. **Distraction**. Hey, if you can stop a fit in its tracks simply by doing a little boogie across the living room floor while singing "Hot Diggity Dog!" at the top of your lungs (not that I would ever sink to *that* level) then, by all means, do it.

2. **A calm facade**. I know you feel like kicking, screaming, and heading to the freezer to down a carton of Häagen-Dazs. But don't. Take a deep breath and keep yourself calm. Perhaps your calmness will rub off on your toddler. Or, if not, at least you'll be better able to deal with the fit when you don't have a carton of ice cream in your hands.

3. **Make believe**. Your toddler can always have exactly what he

wants in fantasyland, right? So, if he's screaming for a cookie ten minutes before dinner, sit down next to him and say, "Let's pretend we're eating a whole pile of cookies!" and then go through the motions of downing cookies and milk together.

4. **Adaptation**. No, you probably don't want your toddler squeezing your entire bottle of Jergens out onto the carpet. But he could, say, play with an empty bottle or help you rub a small squeeze of lotion onto his cute little tootsies.

5. **Friends**. Of course your toddler doesn't want to go take a bath. Why would he when he's having so much fun playing with Mater. But perhaps Mater wants to come take a bath with him? Or watch him from the safe (and dry) perch of the bathroom counter?

6. **Hugging**. My son Joey always needs a hug to pull out of a tantrum—even now that he's six. When he was a toddler, I'd grab him, hold him tight, and say calmly, "I think you need a big hug." Sometimes he'd struggle, but I'd hold tight, and eventually he'd sink into me, sigh, and everything would be okay.

7. **Ignorance**. Yep, that's right. Pretend it isn't happening. Keep an eye on your toddler, but just walk away, find something to distract yourself, and let him throw the fit all by his lonesome.

8. **Crack a joke**. There's nothing like a little humor to defuse a tantrum. Try saying something like, "I know you're better than that silly car seat buckle that you're so mad at, so there's no reason to waste your time yelling at it." Cue smiles, giggles, and done.

9. **Give him a job**. My son Will loves nothing more than "helping" me around the house. So, whenever he is really upset, I distract him with a chore, like helping me put away the (plastic) cups and bowls from the dishwasher or pulling laundry out of the dryer.

10. **Yourself**. There is no law that says you have to play with your kid. So simply say, "I'm not going to play with you if you can't be nice. Let me know when you're ready, and I'll come back."

Section 3: Tantrums in Public

You should also be happy when your kid throws a massive tantrum in public. Not only because it's a ton of fun when your parenting becomes a spectator sport, but also because it never gets old watching your kid kick things that he could easily break and that you would then have to pay for. Or not. Truth is, there is nothing more mortifying, more embarrassing, more ridiculous, and more likely to drive you to doing something crazy yourself (like abandoning a sale at Ann Taylor Loft) than a public toddler tantrum.

A few weeks ago, I took my kids to Target with the sole purpose of hanging out in the toy section in the air-conditioning while I drank a Frappuccino. Because that's how I roll. Everything was going fine until Will started opening one of the Star Wars packages. And since I didn't want to spend forty bucks on a toy that he wasn't even old enough to play with, I took it away from him. Mean mommy, I know. He flipped out. Like, threw himself backwards onto the floor and started throwing all the boxes on the bottom shelf across the aisle. He was putting on a real show, and the myriad of people that appeared out of nowhere to watch were sure enjoying the drama. I, however, was not.

I looked around as people smiled smugly at my predicament, shaking their heads and clearly thinking about how they could've handled the situation better. I wanted to scream at them. To explain that my kids were hot and tired and hungry and in need of a distraction, which was the reason I came to the store in the first place. And I needed a break, too, in the form of an iced vanilla latte with whip! But I didn't yell at anyone. I sheepishly strapped my still-screaming toddler into the cart, grabbed my other two kids, and left posthaste. Ten minutes later, all was back to normal. Will had found something else to play with. My older kids had forgotten our fast retreat from the toy section. And my breathing and stress levels had dropped back to normal.

But seriously, why do kids do that? And pick the worst (read:

most embarrassing) times to boot? Unfortunately, I can't answer that, but I can give you some tools that will help you combat public tantrums—and win.

Eight Tricks for Fighting Public Tantrums

1. **Redirection**. Use your strong grasp of the English language—and logical reasoning—to your advantage to help quell a potential fit. When junior screams, "Me! Cookie!" in the aisle at Target, you can say, "You did have a yummy cookie yesterday at Grandma's house. Can you help me find the applesauce?"

2. **Amusement**. Try a little reverse psychology on your kid and act like you're actually enjoying his fit. Smile and say, "Wow! Look at that fit! You're really getting good at that."

3. **Your legs**. You can leave. Wherever you are, whatever you're doing, you can leave. I remember a day when I had an almost-full grocery cart and one-year-old Kate and three-year-old Joey decided to start whining, hitting, and throwing fits. I warned them, and then I abandoned the cart, scooped a kid under each arm, and left (after notifying the manager that I was so sorry to leave all that food out). It was embarrassing—and I hope I never have to do it again—but a girl's gotta do what a girl's gotta do. (Idea: if you just can't find it in you to attempt another grocery trip or to make the store restock everything, ask the manager if you can put your cart in the walk-in refrigerator and come back for it later when things have calmed down.)

4. **Words**. You simply can't overexplain things to a two-year-old. So, when you're going to playgroup, spend some time before you go, explaining to your kid that you'll be there for an hour and then will go home for a nap. Then, when you get there, explain it again. And when it's five minutes to leave time, explain it again. Then, when it's time to go, your toddler will have had several conversations and opportunities to get used to the idea that he is, in fact, going home and will, in fact, be taking a nap when he gets there.

The Christian Mama's Guide to Parenting a Toddler

5. **Choices**. Your toddler may want that Bob the Builder toy that you said no to, but he probably wants his independence even more. So, give him a choice: either put the toy away himself and come to the shopping cart, or you'll come carry him. Chances are, he'll do it himself. And if he doesn't? Pick him up and put him in the cart. Same result for you, right?

6. **Bribery**. I personally don't have any problem with bribing my kids from time to time. And by time to time, I mean nearly every time I go shopping. Try, "If you can be good at the store, mommy will take you to the park after we put the groceries away." Or, "If we can make it through checkout without whining, mommy will let you have one of these animal cookies in the car."

7. **Denial**. The hilarious Dr. Kevin Lehman once said that his best tantrum-fighting tip is to look at your kid and say loudly, "Wow! Whose kid is that on the floor? His mom must be *so* embarrassed." I love that. Because not only are you taking the attention off of yourself and what you're doing, but you're also helping the kid see that the fit is not affecting you and not going to work.

8. **Goldfish crackers**. I saw a woman in line at Target hand-feeding her tantruming toddler goldfish crackers to keep her quiet while she checked out. The old, pre-parenting me would've been judgmental—imagine feeding your kid a snack because she's throwing a fit—but the new me? I was proud. Proud that this mama knew that nothing starts a tantrum like a blood-sugar drop; therefore, nothing can subdue one like a snack.

The Final Exam

Now it's time for you to prove what you're made of—to show me that all this tantrum talk has sunk in. Put on your "Tantrum Stopper" cape and don your "Supermom" T-shirt, because it's time for your final exam. This is a lab-based test. You will be put in a room with fifteen toddlers, twelve popsicles, four wet wipes, and one talking Elmo doll. If, after twenty minutes, all fifteen children emerge from the room with smiles on their faces and clean hands, you pass. Otherwise, well then, you'll need to read this chapter again.

FOUR

The Food Fight

Getting Your Kid to Eat

My son Joey eats pizza at my mom's house. This wouldn't be strange, except for the fact that he's never touched pizza at home. Too cheesy. And spicy. And waaay too bready. But apparently at my mom's—where Grandma is perfectly understanding about the fact that my son thinks the four food groups are animal crackers, peanut butter, cookies, and frosted animal crackers—the food fight isn't nearly as fun. So, he eats whatever Grandma sets in front of him, even if it's cheesy, spicy, *and* bready.

Of course, at home it's an entirely different story. Joey doesn't eat anything. Okay, that's a lie. He eats a lot of things, but nothing that I deem acceptable as dinner food—or anytime food, for that matter. He absolutely refuses to eat anything that (a) looks mixed up, (b) has touched any sort of sauce or cheese, or (c) has any form of discoloration. Tortillas? Out. They have "brown spots." Scrambled eggs? Nope. They look like they could have cheese in them. Spaghetti? How can you expect a kid to eat a saucy, pasta-y, cheesy mess? Nuh-uh.

My food fight with Joey goes all the way back to the day he turned one and a half. Before that, he was a great eater. When he was a baby, he gobbled down every broccoli-infused puree I set in front of him. As a one-year-old, he chowed down chicken and zucchini and steamed carrots as if they were candy. And even when he was one and a quarter, he happily ate whatever I put on his high chair tray. But then he turned one and a half, and suddenly, he decided that every morsel on his plate was in some way inedible. Chicken chunks? On the floor. Sliced bananas? Thrown to the dog. Broccoli? Yeah, right.

Okay, so I admit that steamed carrots and roasted chicken aren't exactly a Happy Meal, but I was still stunned. I had expected my son to follow in my footsteps and develop a deep and abiding love for anything cheesy or carby, but instead, he had turned into an anti-dairy, anti-carb, anti-deliciousness food tyrant, and I had no idea what to do about it. But I knew I had to do something because I was getting awfully sick of scrubbing mashed bananas off the high chair tray and finding half-chewed chicken tenders behind the cushions.

Types of Toddler Eaters

Before we get into the intricacies of getting a toddler to eat, I thought I'd explain the many types of toddler eaters. This (very professional) list is important so you have a label to stick on your kid next time you're discussing the food fight at playgroup. This will make you seem like a very in-tune mom who really knows her stuff—something that's very important when you're dealing with playgroup politics.

The Supervore

This is the kid you spot at the park, munching on raw Brussels sprouts. When you ask what he's eating (thinking that perhaps it's a Brussels sprout–shaped cookie), his mama explains that little Junior just eats any vegetable he can get his hands on—along with anything else she happens to put on his high chair tray. Tikka masala? He loves the stuff. Steamed grouper? His favorite. Oh, and—isn't this cute—little Junior asked for tofu stir-fry with cauliflower for his birthday dinner. Ummmmm, yeah. So, I've heard rumors that kids like this exist, but I have yet to meet one in person. And if you do manage to figure out how to get your kid to eat steamed okra without a major meltdown, my suggestion is that you call TLC right away. You may just end up as the next reality show star. *Supernanny of the Dinner Table* or something cool like that.

The Carnivore

These kids love themselves some meat, which would be a good thing...if the meat they craved was broiled fish or skinless boneless chicken breasts. But more often than not, carnivore toddlers love themselves some cut-up hot dogs. And bacon. And ham. And, well, if you're lucky, they may gobble down some deep-fried and battered chicken strips for good measure. My son Joey is like this. He would eat bacon-wrapped sausage patties until his Superman costume got tight, but if I offered him steamed fish—or (gasp!) a hunk of grilled chicken—he would probably rather starve.

The Fruitivore

So, fruit's healthy, right? Yes! And it's great if all your kid wants to do is eat strawberries and blueberries and grapes that have been carefully cut in half and double inspected by you to make sure one half isn't bigger than the other. But let me just warn you of a common side effect of fruitivorism: fruit is a natural laxative. And when you give a kid four platesful of natural laxatives in one day, then more likely than not, you're going to have some diaper trouble later that night. Just sayin'.

The Carbivore

This is the second most common type of toddler eater, surpassed only by the very prevalent "cheesivore." Carbivores chow

Cheerios (no milk) before breakfast, then round it out with toast (no butter) and frozen waffles (no syrup). For lunch, they'll ask for PB & J (no PB . . . or J) with a side of saltine crackers. And for dinner, they'll have mashed potatoes (no gravy), biscuits (no honey), and pound cake (yes, please, on the whipped cream!). The good news about carbivores is that you'll never have to worry that they're eating enough calories—they are.

The Cheesivore

Nearly 50 percent of toddlers (and 30 percent of adults) are cheesivores. Cheeseivores will eat (almost) anything as long as it's covered in a thick layer of melted cheese. So, while broccoli is a no-no, broccoli au gratin with an extra layer of melted cheddar on top is a favorite. If you have a cheesivore on your hands, you may want to get a Costco membership, because cheese is expensive, and, well, let's be honest, if you have it around the house, you may as well put a little on your own broccoli too.

The Sugarvore

Sugarvores will do anything for something sweet—and that means that if you want them to take two teensy tiny bites of that broiled asparagus, you'd better have a giant chocolate chip cookie dangling in front of their noses. The good thing about sugarvores is that you can usually get them to eat anything, but the bad news is that you'll have to give them a gummy bear for doing it.

So, How Do You Get Your Toddler to Eat?

After noticing that my son (a) ate pizza happily at my mom's house without complaining, and (b) threw massive fits pretty much every time I put anything (including pizza) on his plate, I realized there was a teensy tiny chance that I was part of the problem. Remember what I said earlier about toddlers asserting their independence? Well, kids are much smarter than we give them credit for, and my son had some-how figured out that I cared about what he ate. And since I cared about it, he was going to do anything in his power to control it—because that's what one-and-a-half-year-olds do. It was time for a game plan.

Of course, I had no idea where to even start, so I asked my sister, Alisa, who is a real, live registered dietitian with a fancy schmancy *RD* after her name, to give me some toddler eating tips and ideas. Here's what she said:

Ten Rules (Okay, Guidelines) for Mealtime
1. **Don't make eating an issue—even if it is**. Your kid is smart. He knows you want him to eat. So your job is to pretend you couldn't care less if he eats the asparagus on his plate.
2. **Act as though the asparagus is candy**. Rave about the food to your husband. Say, "*Mmmm*" with every bite you take. Ask for seconds of the "delicious asparagus."
3. **Be consistent with your rules**. If your rule is that your kid has to eat at least one bite of everything, then make sure he eats one bite of everything at every meal. If your rule is that your kid loses his tray if he throws food, then take away the tray every single time he throws food.
4. **Include your kid in dinner table discussion**, even if he can't talk well enough to hold up his end of the convo.
5. **Experiment with new things**. Kids get stuck in food ruts very, very easily. It's important to expose them to new foods, even if there is no way they're going to touch them. I made it a goal to try to include one new or interesting thing—whether it was a new kind of fruit, a new veggie, or a new shape of pasta—on my son's dinner plate at least one time per week.
6. **Always serve at least one thing they'll definitely like**. I know I just told you to expose your kid to new foods, but it's equally important to make mealtime enjoyable for them. So make sure there's at least one (somewhat healthy) thing on the table at every meal that you know your kid loves.

7. **Model good eating habits**. How's this for a super-annoying eating fact: kids tend to like to eat what their parents eat. So if you survive on sprinkles, gummy bears, and chocolate kisses, your kid will probably think that's a perfectly reasonable diet. So, whenever you load your kid's plate up with veggies, toss a few on your plate as well. (This goes for Daddy too! He's definitely not off the hook when it comes to the butternut squash.)

8. **Let your kid be the chef**. My daughter Kate has refused to even let lasagna enter her field of vision since she was tiny. But, last week when she was helping me cook dinner for a friend, Kate noticed that lasagna was really just spaghetti in layers. Smart kid, eh? And since spaghetti is one of her favorite foods, she happily ate lasagna that night.

9. **Involve your kids in the planning**. Look through cookbooks together or spend a few minutes together on Pinterest, scoping out recipes that look good.

10. **Help them to rise to the occasion**. My friend told me that every few weeks, she does a random "fancy" dinner where she lights candles, sets the table with china, and serves water in wine glasses. She says it's amazing how her kids rise to the occasion—both with manners and eating—when they get the opportunity to act like princes and princesses.

Ten (Almost) Surefire Toddler Meals

As much as you'd love for your kid to eat veggies and lean protein and whole grains with every meal, that's just not going to happen. But you'd still rather your kid's nutritional intake went beyond raisins and goldfish crackers. I've lived with a super-picky toddler eater, and I know the food fight can be exhausting, so I asked Alisa to give me ten (almost) surefire toddler meals that are (pretty) healthy and super yummy. (Bonus: all ten of these passed through at least one of my kids' yuck-o-meters with flying colors.)

1. **Dippin' Dinner**. Load a plate up with "dippers"—grilled chicken tenders, stringless snow peas, thin slices of cheese, cucumber sticks, whole-wheat crackers. Then, squeeze a small amount of several dips on a plate (try ranch dressing, yogurt, hummus, applesauce, ketchup, and barbecue sauce) and have your toddler experiment with his or her favorite combinations.

2. **Mama McMuffins**. Brown chicken sausage and finely chopped bell peppers in a skillet. Scramble in eggs. Layer on top of whole-wheat English muffins, and melt cheese on top. (Hint: You can take the peppers out if you want, but I wouldn't, because they probably won't notice them underneath the cheese and mixed with the sausage chunks.)

3. **Polka-Dot Pasta**. Toss cooked pasta with a smidge of butter, a half cup of peas, a sprinkle of parmesan, and a squeeze of lemon. I know lemon and parmesan sounds a bit crazy, but I promise it's good.

4. **PB&J Waffle Sandies**. Plop PB&J (or if you want to pass it off as "dessert," PB & Nutella) between two toasted whole-wheat waffles.

5. **Turkey Sliders**. Mix a pound of ground turkey with half of a finely chopped red or yellow pepper and a dash of salt. Make into mini patties and grill until completely cooked. Melt a slice of Monterrey Jack cheese on top (which serves to hide the peppers from curious eyes) and serve on whole-wheat slider buns (look in the bread aisle at your supermarket).

6. **Cauliflower Mac & Cheese**. My friend Staci gave me this recipe, and I admit I was a bit skeptical. I'm not a huge fan of cauliflower myself, and I couldn't imagine that I would be able to mix it into mac & cheese without argument. But I was wrong. All you do is take a head of cauliflower and pop it into your food processor and puree until smooth. Add a half cup of the puree (freeze the rest) to your favorite mac & cheese recipe (cooked or homemade) and *voilà*! Kate and Will asked

for seconds. Joey doesn't eat anything "noodle-y" or cheesy, so he ate the cauliflower plain. Strange kid, right?

7. **Crunchy Maple Salmon**. Mix a quarter cup of mild mustard with a quarter cup of pure maple syrup. Place one pound of fresh salmon in an ovenproof dish and spread the mustard/syrup mixture on top. Sprinkle with half a cup of whole-wheat Panko breadcrumbs and bake at 350 degrees for twenty minutes or until tender. Your kid will love the sweetness of the syrup and the crunch from the breadcrumbs. (And the brainpower delivered from the omega-3s definitely can't hurt when it comes to teaching him his colors and shapes.)

8. **Mini Bean Burritos**. Mix one can of refried beans with one can of black beans and a quarter cup of Monterey Jack cheese. Spread on whole-wheat tortillas and wrap into small burritos. Warm up in the microwave for forty seconds.

9. **Monster Noodles**. Boil spinach-flavored pasta with chopped asparagus or broccoli. Toss with a quarter cup of pesto, half a cup of light cream cheese, and half a cup of milk. Sprinkle with parmesan.

10. **Greek Wraps**. Make a simple, kid-friendly tzatziki by grating half of a peeled cucumber into one cup of plain Greek yogurt. Add salt, pepper, and garlic salt to taste. Wrap small chunks of chicken, diced tomatoes, and black olives in whole-wheat pita bread, and let your kid dip her wrap into the tzatziki. I know, I know. Sounds fancy. But it has bread, yogurt, and olives. What's not to love?

Ten Pretty Healthy Toddler Snacks

Getting a toddler to snack is easy—as long you don't mind giving her chocolate chip cookies and goldfish crackers whenever she's hungry. Getting your toddler to snack on healthy things is a bit harder. Here are a few (pretty) healthy snacks to try with your toddler.

1. **Bunnies on a Log.** Spread a thin layer of peanut butter on a banana; then cover it with Annie's whole-wheat flavored bunny crackers.

2. **Cheese Crisps.** Make crunchy yummy crackers out of cheese . . . yep, just cheese. Sprinkle shredded Monterey Jack or Cheddar cheese in a small circle on a piece of parchment paper spread on a cookie sheet. Bake at 350 degrees for twenty minutes until brown and melty. Let cool for one hour.

3. **Pumpkin Pie Sundae.** Mix three tablespoons of pureed pumpkin and a dash of cinnamon into vanilla yogurt. Top with sliced almonds.

4. **Going Bananas Smoothie.** Dump one cup of milk, two table-spoons of Ovaltine, one banana, and two tablespoons of peanut butter into the blender. Blend until smooth.

5. **Little Dippers.** Stringless snap peas and bell pepper strips dipped in hummus.

6. **Sunny-Side Ups.** Graham crackers smothered with Sunbutter (sunflower seed butter).

7. **Pickles in a Blanket.** Wrap sliced deli turkey around petite sweet pickles and secure with a blob of mustard.

8. **Going Bananas.** Dip sliced bananas and strawberries in plain yogurt.

9. **Cheesysauce.** Have your kid dip mild cheddar cheese slices into unsweetened applesauce.

10. **Cold Fruit Soup.** Blend one ripe mango or six ripe strawber-ries with one cup of plain yogurt and half a cup of apple juice until smooth. Pour into a bowl and plop in some pieces of strawberry or some fresh blueberries to make it chunky.

Choking

I'm not going to sugarcoat it: choking is scary. It's probably on the top-five list of every mother's biggest nightmares. Even worse, it happens a lot—especially with toddlers who haven't quite learned how to chew large chunks of food and often shovel more food than they can handle into their mouths. You can't be too careful. Okay, so you probably don't need to show up at your third grader's Halloween party to cut the grapes in half, but when your child is under three, you have every right to turn yourself into the choking hazard police.

The biggest choking risks are typically things that are round (i.e., exactly the same size as a kid's windpipe) and hard, but any food can be a choking hazard if it's shoveled into your kid's mouth by the handful. The best thing you can do is be super-vigilant about what—and how much—your kid is putting into his or her mouth. It also may be a good idea to take a toddler CPR course (I found one offered through the local fire station) just to make sure you know what to do if your kid does choke. Aside from that, here's a list of the biggest choking hazards (thanks to the American Academy of Pediatrics [AAP]) and what to do to cut the risk:

- Hot dogs: cut them into quarters, lengthwise.
- Grapes: cut them into half lengthwise.
- Marshmallows: cut big ones into small chunks; cut mini ones in half lengthwise.
- Popcorn: avoid giving your kid popcorn until he or she is at least three.
- String cheese: split in half lengthwise.
- Baby carrots: cut into quarters lengthwise.
- Celery sticks: use a knife to cut off the stringy side—the long, stringy stalks can get caught in your kid's throat.
- Hard, round candies (like peppermints, Tootsie Rolls, hard licorice): cut or break in half lengthwise.
- Chunks of meat (chicken, beef, turkey): cut into small chunks (less than a quarter inch in diameter).
- Cheese cubes: cut into thin slices.
- Balloons: Okay, so balloons aren't a food, but since the AAP names them as the number-one choking hazard for

toddlers, I'd be remiss not to add them to the list. Balloons are a ton of fun when they're blown up, but once one pops, make sure to take it away from your kid immediately.

Throwing Food

You know that orange lump on your kid's plate? Well, to you it may look a lot like the sweet potatoes you spent two hours steaming, mashing, and seasoning this afternoon, but to your kid it's a big ole pile of edible, smearable fun. And whatever portion your kid doesn't manage to smear across his high chair tray and all over his brand-new Gap T-shirt, he'll drop onto the floor. Wait. Strike that. He'll throw it onto the floor in big heaping mounds that spread out during their descent and manage to make their way into every nook and cranny, including the tiny crack between the front and the back of your upholstered dining chair.

Every one-and-a-half-year-old tries his or her hand at the food-throwing game at least once. Why? Well, mostly because it's a lot of fun. And if you really think about it, you'd probably rather throw your great-aunt's rutabaga casserole on the floor than eat it too. But seeing as how throwing soft, sticky orange wads of goo is generally frowned upon in polite (and even impolite) company, it's probably a good idea to teach your kid that throwing food on the floor is a no-no.

So, how do you do that? Well, that's easy. When little Junior decides to throw a giant wad of lasagna onto your mother-in-law's soft peach carpet, you smile sweetly and say in your most singsongy voice, "Silly baby! That's not a good idea to throw food!" Oh, wait? That doesn't work? Yeah, I tried that too. When my son Joey decided that food in general was a fun thing to throw but not a fun thing to eat, I gave him a sweet talking-to. Then a stern talking-to. Then I whined. Then I yelled. And guess what? None of it worked. Turns out that lectures don't really work with one-and-a-half-year-olds.

So, after another bowl-of-spaghetti-on-the-floor incident, I pulled out the big guns: I called my mom. And she told me to take his plate away. Just like that. She told me to say something like, "Oh no! Looks like you don't want your dinner!" and to move his plate away from him and then to continue on with our dinnertime conversation.

I'm sure you know what I was thinking when my mom said that: what if he gets hungry? What if he ends up eating only white food for dinner and no green food or orange food and then he doesn't get enough vitamins and minerals and he starts to lose weight and gets diagnosed with scurvy at his next doctor's visit? I would never take my baby's food away! He was a growing boy. There had to be another way.

So we plodded on. I continued making delicious and well-balanced meals, and Joey continued to throw them all on the floor. Finally, in a moment of desperation, after he threw an entire plateful of lentil stew on the floor, I gave in. I took his high chair tray away. I set it on the table out of arm's reach. I took a deep breath and said, "Uh-oh! Looks like you don't want your dinner!" and then I continued eating my own steaming bowl of lentils while trying to keep a happy face. I felt so guilty—there I was, gobbling down a hot and hearty dinner, while my growing son sat there stunned—without a bite on his plate.

It wasn't an easy night. My son whined and cried in his high chair, and I almost gave in and made him a PB & J. I had to call my mom twice to get a little "stay strong" pep talk. I worried all night that my son was never going to eat again. But guess what? He did eat again. The very next morning. And get this: he ate his entire breakfast without throwing a thing. Not even the big bowl of applesauce that would've certainly been his main form of breakfast entertainment had we not had our little "don't throw food" lesson the night before.

I'd like to say he never threw a speck of food again, but that would be a lie. We had to repeat the above lesson every two or three months until he turned two and realized that throwing food wasn't nearly as fun as throwing fits about wanting cookies. But I digress. My point in all this? Yes, your kid will throw food. Yes, it's going to irritate you. But no, you're never ever going to convince your kid not to throw food by lecturing, cajoling, or talking. You have to take action. And taking away his food for just one meal is a natural consequence.

Ending the Food Fight . . . Or Not

Let me give it to you straight. Your food fight with your kid will probably not be over . . . ever. My kid is six and he still doesn't voluntarily eat anything that's not (a) salted meat, (b) covered in chocolate, or (c) colored bright blue by artificial coloring. That said, things have gotten better since he got out of the terrible twos. I no longer have to worry about him throwing peas on the floor (he quietly slides them into his napkin and feeds them to the dog) or smearing sweet potatoes in his hair (that would mean he'd have to take a shower before bed, and he would *not* want that to happen). So, see? It gets better! Or at least less messy.

As soon as you get done scrubbing that spaghetti sauce off of your wallpaper, it's time for a mama break. Next up, we're talking about how to teach your kid how to live a healthy lifestyle from the time he's little. Which means you may need to reconsider the Costco-sized bag of M&M's you just bought for potty training bribes. Raisins work just as well . . . at least according to the non-parents who write parenting articles.

FIVE

Living a Healthy Lifestyle

*Teaching Your Toddler How to
Live Healthy from an Early Age*

When my kids were babies, my entire motivation for exercising and eating healthy stemmed from a desire to button my jeans. I was honestly getting a bit tired of wearing elastic-waist pants, of people asking how far along I was when I was no longer pregnant, and of having to wear Spanx to even look somewhat presentable. So, I exercised. And ate totally non-delicious things, like raw spinach and broiled fish. And I eventually (okay, *finally*) lost that baby weight.

And then I quit.

I got busy with my toddler, and my life and my trips out with the jogging stroller became few and far between. And the idea of eating one more spinach salad without croutons made me want to hurl. So, I went back to my old, unmotivated ways. And while I certainly was able to still button my (biggest) jeans, my motivation to eat and stay healthy was gone.

Enter my sister Alisa. The registered dietitian, the former college athlete, the girl who not only lost her baby weight but has kept it off for more than three years. And leave it to her to find the one (and only) thing that would motivate me to start exercising and eating well again: my kids. Alisa reminded me that my kids watch me. They watch what I do, what I eat, how I take care of myself. And if they grow up watching their mom sit around eating Ding Dongs washed down by Orange Crush all day, they may start to think that's a good idea.

Talk about motivation! I think every mom out there has an innate desire to see her kids grow up to live healthy lives. And while very few moms have an innate desire to kill themselves in Strike class, the thought that your kids are watching every healthy (or unhealthy) choice you make is probably enough to motivate you to drag your Spanx-loving patootie out of the gym's café and actually go to workout class. At least it's enough for me.

So, with all that said, I asked Alisa—the girl who motivated me— to give me a few pointers on how to set a healthy-living example for my kids. And I'm sharing them with you because I want some company in Strike class. (And no, not because misery loves company, but because I need someone to stand in the back with me and help me figure out how to kick and punch at the same time.)

Unleashing Your Inner Gym Rat (and Ratlets)

I know you're legs are still burning from the 459 times you played "Ring Around the Rosie" yesterday. I know you want nothing more at this moment than for your kid to sit for three minutes so you can catch your breath. But having a toddler who is super-active is a good thing. In fact, the National Association for Sport and Physical Education says that a toddler should not be inactive for more than an hour at a time, except when he's sleeping. So, sadly, that dream you have of an afternoon pajama party while quietly reading books and watching Disney movies may have to go. (But seriously, it's not like your kid was actually going to sit for that long anyway.)

There's a whole slew of reasons why it's important to encourage your toddler to be active. And most of them are the same reasons you should be exercising yourself. As a general rule, humans who exercise are healthier. And healthy humans are not only able to button those jeans but are also less likely to get sick, more likely to be happy, and more likely even to sleep better. Which is good for toddlers and toddler mommies.

And if that isn't enough motivation for you, Mr. Google told me that kids who like to engage in active play when they're young are more likely to stay active as adults. And that means your kids may just end up being among those people who actually like to go to the gym. Or who run 58-mile races for fun. You never know.

The good news is this: it's really not very hard to get a toddler moving. I'm sure you can attest to the fact that it's what they do. Naturally. All day long. All you have to do is try not to stifle it while you stay caffeinated enough to keep up. Alisa and I collaborated to come up with several fun and easy ways to keep your toddler moving—and to utilize all that toddler energy (and maybe burn some calories yourself in the process).

Ten Ways to Keep Your Toddler Active

1. **Be a zoo**. Imitate as many animals as you can think of together. Walk like a penguin; crawl like a cat; hop like a kangaroo.
2. **Play Simon Says . . . with an active twist**. Instead of telling your kid that Simon says to blink his eyes, tell him that Simon says to hop twenty times and then run to the slide and back.
3. **Row, row, row your arms**. Sit facing each other, holding hands. Rock back and forth and sing "Row, Row, Row Your Boat."

Then repeat it, like, two hundred times until your arms start to burn or your toddler falls asleep, whichever comes first.

4. **Blast music, and have a dance party.** Bonus points for making a dance video that you can share with grandma.

5. **Get sporty.** Play T-ball or soccer in the backyard. (So what if your kid thinks he can score a touchdown by running around the bases backwards and doing a somersault onto the pitching mound? At least he's moving.)

6. **Go swimming.** Nothing motivates a kid to really start moving like the ability to splash around in a pool. And nothing motivates a mama to really start moving like having to put on a swimsuit.

7. **Go on a family "hike."** Leave your stroller at home, and go on a neighborhood jaunt. Even better: talk about God's creation as you walk, and put a spiritual spin on your exercise.

8. **Enroll your kid in a class.** While it's certainly not necessary to start your kid in soccer class or gymnastics when he's two, let's be honest: sometimes it's nice to pay someone else to run around and chase your kid while you drink a mocha. Oh, wait. You're supposed to be active too. I meant that sometimes it's nice to pay someone else to run around and chase your kid while you do crunches in your car.

9. **Limit screen time.** Don't hate the messenger here—I know how much you love your morning appointment with the Wiggles. I don't see anything wrong with occasionally using the TV as a babysitter so you can make dinner (or just sit on the couch and veg), but I also think you'll agree with me when I say that the more time your kids—and you—spend in front of the TV, the less active you are.

10. **Just go outside and play.** My kids just feel happier outside, and if I'm being honest, as long as it's not 9 billion degrees out, I feel pretty happy out of doors as well. Fight the urge to stay inside all day, and take your kids (and yourself) out to just run and be free.

Become a (Health) Foodie

My sister, Alisa, is a registered dietitian, so she studies food for a living. When I asked her the best way to get kids to eat healthy, I assumed she'd tell me about tofu or the evils of a high-carb diet. But instead, she told me that her number one suggestion to her clients is this: teach your kids (and yourself) about real food.

What exactly does that mean? I mean, I'm pretty laid-back about my kids' food choices, and even I don't let them eat fake plastic food from the kitchen toy set. But according to Alisa, fake foods—or highly processed foods full of chemicals and preservatives—are becoming more and more common in our culture. And most parents feed them to their kids unknowingly on a regular basis.

Sadly, research is showing that fake foods can be blamed for a lot of our diet woes these days. She says that one of the most important ways to teach your kids to eat healthy is not to educate them on calories or fat grams or carbs or fats, but simply to expose them to real, natural foods. She said that by teaching them to eat the foods God designed for us and that our bodies were designed to eat, we can make healthy food choices without a lot of stress.

To help illustrate this point, Alisa lined her counter with a packet of strawberry Kool-Aid, a bag of strawberry fruit snacks (the kind with "real fruit juice added"), a bottle of 100 percent apple-strawberry juice, and a bowl of fresh strawberries. She had me look at the spectrum of strawberry foods and put them in order from healthiest to least healthy. And I did it in four seconds flat. Go, me! But the truth is that I think anyone reading this book can easily tell you that fresh strawberries are healthier than strawberry Kool-Aid. And likewise, as we make food choices for ourselves and our kids, it's pretty simple to assess whether something is a "real" food or a heavily processed "fake" food.

Alisa says that her definition of real foods is things that either are grown in the ground, like fruits and veggies and grains, or things that come from animals, like meats, fish, eggs, and dairy products.

Talk to your toddler about how God makes fruits and veggies for us to eat. And (unless you're vegan) how He gives us animals to provide for our needs too. It just makes sense that the majority of what you eat and feed your kid should be these kinds of foods.

This isn't to say that your kid can't ever have a packet of fruit snacks or a bag of chips, because there is always room in a healthy diet for the occasional treat. But Alisa firmly believes that if all moms made a concentrated effort to feed their kids real foods the majority of the time, we'd have a healthier society in general. And I tend to agree with her.

So start thinking about the food you eat and buy. Does most of it come from a farm, or is it made in a laboratory? When you look at the ingredients in your food, can you pronounce them, or do they require a PhD in food science to know what they are? The scary thing is that when we eat a lot of these fake-out foods, we start to develop a taste for them. On the other hand, if you feed your toddler a diet of "real" food from the get-go, he'll probably develop a taste for it.

Five Tips for Getting Your Toddler to Develop a Taste for Real Food

1. **Go Local**. Take an excursion to a local farmer's market or farm and talk about all the amazing foods God created for us. If you can, sample fresh produce or pick up a new vegetable to try for dinner.
2. **Plant a garden**. My niece Haddie, who acts as though she might die if you put something green on her dinner plate, is so proud of what she's grown in her backyard that she now munches on fresh spinach leaves when she's playing outside. And I have to admit that I am much more motivated to whip up fresh veggies for dinner when they are ready and ripe, right in my backyard.
3. **Cook with your kids**. Kids get excited about the food

they cook, so let your toddler lend you a hand as you wash produce or stir ingredients. One of my favorite kids-in-the-kitchen tools is a kid-safe knife from the Curious Chef (www.curiouschef.com). They cut food (and not fingers), which is a good thing, for obvious reasons.

4. **Don't let pickiness discourage you.** I think we've all heard that it can take ten to fifteen times seeing a new food for a picky eater to be willing to eat it. I totally disagree with that assertion, because I guarantee I gave Joey broccoli at least 128 times before he decided it was edible. But I kept trying. And my hard work paid off last week when Joey announced that broccoli was now—wait for it—his favorite vegetable.

5. **Talk about food.** Next time you make yourself a green smoothie, tell your toddler that you're excited to drink it because you know how good it is for your body. I'm guessing your little Incredible Hulk may just want to try some to add to his own bodybuilding prowess. Those carrots? They give you Superman vision. The beets? Pretty princess anti-oxidants. If you think hard enough, you'll be able to find a superpower for just about every healthy food you want them to eat.

. . . .

Time-Out for Mom

For When You're Working to Set a Healthy Example for Your Child

"'Because he loves me,' says the Lord, 'I will rescue him;
I will protect him, for he acknowledges my name.
He will call on me, and I will answer him;
I will be with him in trouble,
I will deliver him and honor him.
With long life I will satisfy him
and show him my salvation.'" (Psalm 91:14–16)

I love You, Lord! I truly and wholeheartedly do! And You have promised that You will answer the prayers of and deliver those who acknowledge Your name. And I do! I know that You are the living God and the creator of the heavens and the earth. And I pray that I will be able to live a life worthy of Your calling, setting a healthy and righteous example for my family. Amen.

Be A Healthy Living Role Model

"Practice what we preach." It's easy to spout off adages like that and assume that you'll inspire others and yourself to do the right thing, but actually *doing* the things that you want your kids to do? That's harder. Because let's be honest: unhealthy choices are often easier. It's easier to give your kid a packet of fruit snacks than to rinse and cut fresh strawberries. It's easier to grab a bag of Lays and some M&M's instead of taking the time to make yourself a chicken salad. It's easier to stay home than to go to the gym. It's easier. But easier isn't always better. And the things you do right now are setting the example for the choices your toddler will make in the future.

So next time you grab for that soda, remember that your kid is watching. And your kid will one day have to make the choice between soda and water. Which do you want him to choose?

SIX

Bedtime Battles

*Helping Your Toddler
Become a Great Sleeper*

I once heard an urban legend about a toddler who slept in until 8:00 a.m. every morning and then woke up, climbed out of her big-girl bed, slipped off her Pull-Up, and went to the kitchen to fix herself a bowl of cereal. But all this is unsubstantiated. I have yet to see any real proof that such a toddler has ever existed.

My personal experience with toddler sleep patterns is more in line with the truth. At least the truth as I know it. All three of my kids were decent sleepers by the time they hit that one-year-old mark. I wasn't spending hours rocking them to sleep or dragging myself out of bed at 2:00 a.m. to nurse, but let me assure you that "decent" sleeping by toddler standards is nothing like what you would have considered "decent" sleeping a few years ago. Because try as you might, the idea of a mom under the covers at 9:00 a.m. is something that only exists in fairy tales and when Grandma comes to visit.

After some gossipmonger told us about the aforementioned super-toddler who made her own bowl of cereal and then played quietly so her parents could sleep, my husband and I decided to test it out with our then two-year-old Joey. I set up a cute little table outside of his room with a juice box and a dry bowl of Kix (even I wasn't naive enough to risk letting him pour his own milk) and enthusiastically walked him through the steps. He was going to wake up at whatever ungodly hour he wanted to wake up, but instead of coming to get me, he was going to quietly eat his cereal while looking at board books at the table. We even practiced.

The next morning, I heard the pitter-patter of little feet at 4:43 a.m. He was coming to ask me if it was time to eat his cereal. Then, at 4:52, he came to tell me that his cereal tasted good. At 5:03, I learned that he spilled two Kix on the floor. And at 5:07, he came down to let me know he was done with his Kix and was ready for me to get up and play with him. The idea that had seemed so brilliant the night before had bought me twenty-four extra minutes of interrupted sleep.

I wish I could tell you that I've cracked the code to toddler sleeping and taught Joey how to scramble his own eggs each morning without dragging me out of bed to do it for him. But I haven't. My kids are in elementary school now, and they still wake up before seven every morning. And while they are perfectly capable of making their own cereal (and even pouring their own milk), they rarely do it. Instead, they come and ask me for waffles.

The key to being successful with the toddler bedtime battle is keeping your expectations very, very low. Expect to be woken up at o'dark o'clock. Expect to walk up the stairs seventeen times to tell your toddler to stop throwing his lovey out of the crib and go to sleep. (Which, on the bright side, means you don't have to go to the gym the next day.) Expect whining. Expect tears. And then, if by some fluke of nature your kid decides to fall asleep during his bedtime story or sleep until 6:15, you'll feel as though you hit the sleep jackpot. Aren't I encouraging?

Now that your expectations have been appropriately set, it's time to go into battle. Arm yourself with a good bedtime story and a sippy cup of water because it's time to get your toddler sleeping. At least decently well.

Bedtime Routines

My husband is the kind of person who waits until he gets to the airport to see where he's going to go on vacation. He just selects the flight that looks as though it's going to the most exciting place and worries about minor details like where he's going to sleep and how he's going to get back once he's there. If you know me at all, you know that his fly-by-the-seat-of-his-Calvin-Kleins stuff drives me crazy because I am the kind of person who plans my summer vacation in January. A year and a half in advance. And then I worry that my late planning may result in me missing some of the best early-bird specials.

Anyway, with our opposing personalities in mind, I'm sure you can imagine how he reacted when I suggested implementing a bedtime routine. Because any sentence that includes the words "schedule" or "routine" or "plan ahead" automatically results in him hyperventilating. Or something almost that extreme. But I put my foot down because all the parenting magazines said bedtime routines were "in" and I always do what's popular and trendy and hip. Well, that and the magazines said that bedtime routines can really help create consistent sleep habits. And we were desperate.

The idea was genius. And I take all the credit. Creating a bedtime routine was really the best thing we did for our kids (and ourselves) because once they got into the groove, the consistent tried-and-true plan really helped them settle down and fall asleep. And stay asleep. I'm pretty sure even my husband would agree that bedtime routines trump bedtime not-routines. Not that I said,

"I told you so" or anything immature like that. Anyway, here are some of the things we did to make sure our toddlers had a consistent nighttime routine.

Six Tips for Creating a Successful Toddler Bedtime Routine

Start bedtime early. At our house, we actually start our bedtime routine right after dinner. This isn't (only) because we're chomping at the bit to get the kids down, but because my kids always seem to be their crankiest right before bedtime. So we've gotten into the habit of doing something active together—like a walk outside or a half hour playing in the backyard—right after dinner. Our kids really look forward to these times, and it's a great way to finish off the day doing something fun together.

Don't force bath time. There are lots of people who will tell you that bedtime baths are a great way to help your kids wind down. And that may be true—for people whose kids haven't figured out that if they stand up in the tub and pour a bucket of water over the edge, mommy and daddy will scream and throw towels. But if you are getting a bit tired of spending your evenings wading in Lake Bathroom Floor, then you may want to nix baths from the bedtime routine. I've found that morning baths—or even showers—tend to be much less stressful.

Incorporate God into your routine. Finish off every day with Jesus. We read from *The Jesus Storybook Bible* to our kids every night, but if that's above your toddler's head, you can still make God an important part of your bedtime routine. Sing songs, read Christian-based children's books, or do a family round-robin prayer.

Choose a spot for stories and prayers. Part of making a routine is making it consistent. And that goes for location as well. We've designated our upstairs couch as bedtime central.

We keep our kids' prayer book and Bible in a basket next to the couch and leave a soft blanket for each kid tossed over the couch. The kids know that once they have their pj's on and their teeth brushed, they should head to the couch, snuggle in, and wait there for us to join them.

Let your kid wind down on his own. My son Joey always needs self-soothing time after his mommy-daddy soothing time. When he was a toddler, I found that when I did the whole lights-out-and-silence thing right after our bedtime routine, he'd start to cry. He needed a transition. I started putting a few board books in his crib and playing a soothing CD in his room, and he'd spend a few minutes "reading" by himself and then drift off.

Break your own rules from time to time. Every once in a while, we do something totally out of character (for me) and break the bedtime routine. Last week, we packed pj's and headed to the pool for dinner and an evening swim. Afterward, we showered the kids down, put them in their pj's, and let them fall asleep in the car. My kids loved it.

Morning Routines

I'm pretty certain my kids have conspired to make sure I am up before 6:00 every morning for the rest of my life. They've had a good run at it and even managed to make it look somewhat coincidental that a different child and a different reason wakes me up every morning, but I'm onto them. I've figured out their scheme.

Joey, of course, is the ringleader. Not only is he the keeper of the spreadsheet (I haven't found it yet, but it's got to be hidden somewhere in his room), but he's also the one who assigns morning wake-ups based on my mood and my schedule. I can just hear him at one of their secret meetings now:

"Okay, Kate, you haven't gotten up to watch TV at 4:30 a.m. for a few weeks now, so let's try that one again tonight. Just make sure to throw a knock-down-drag-out fit and insist that it looks like morning to you when they try to take you to bed. And Will, you're our secret weapon because they still watch you with that video monitor contraption. So start screaming, "Mama! Milk!" at 5:15 tomorrow morning. Then bump it up by ten minutes every day for a week. I'm going to throw a before-six pancake request into the mix on Tuesday, and we're all covered for the week."

The problem here is that even though I've figured out their scheme, I have yet to figure out how to stop it. Because while they are a well-oiled machine of early-morning wake-ups, I'm usually too groggy at that time in the morning to even know what's happening. And by the time my coffee has kicked in, they're usually sitting quietly with innocent smiles on their faces, acting as if it's the most natural thing in the world to be up before Starbucks opens. I'm telling you, people, there's a reason Starbucks doesn't open until 5:00 a.m. It's just not normal human behavior to be up at that hour.

Speaking of normal human behavior, you may be tempted to try to put your toddler to bed later in hopes that he'll sleep later. But as logical as this sounds, it never works. Not only because your toddler is clearly scheming against you to make sure you never sleep and therefore will do anything and everything to continue the pattern, but also because every sleep expert I've ever met says that the later you put kids to bed, the earlier they get up. And while I'm not a sleep expert, I can tell you from personal experience that this tends to be true.

Conspiracy theory aside, there are some things you can to do buy yourself a few more minutes under the covers. Nothing I say will ever buy you a good old-fashioned, in-bed-until-noon sleep-in, but I do have a few tricks to help you embrace those early toddler mornings—and possibly grab a few extra zzzz's in the process.

Time-Out for Mom

For When You're Exhausted, Worn Down, or Just Plain Tired

> "Do you not know?
> Have you not heard?
> The LORD is the everlasting God,
> the Creator of the ends of the earth.
> He will not grow tired or weary,
> and his understanding no one can fathom." (Isaiah 40:28)

Everlasting God, I thank You that when I am exhausted and worn down, You are still God. You never grow weary and will be my protector every day of my life. I thank You for being the one and only thing I can count on. Amen.

Eight Things You Can Do to Embrace Those Early Toddler Mornings

Let your toddler stay in bed for a while. You may think it's part of the super-mom code to fly out of bed the instant you hear "Ba! Ba! La La La!" on the monitor. But it's not. In fact, it's perfectly acceptable to leave your (happy) baby in his crib for twenty minutes while you doze.

Stock up your toddler's crib. Give your toddler a reason to want to stay in his crib. Sneak in after bedtime and put a few board books or toys and a sippy cup of water in with him so he wakes up to a fun morning surprise.

Leave the shades open. Waking up in a pitch-black room can be scary, even for adults who know monsters don't exist. Leave your toddler's shades open so he can wake up to natural morning light. Good morning, sunshine!

Leave the shades closed. Of course, some babies need pitch-black darkness to sleep, so if the morning light seems to be waking them up, pick up some blackout shades, and leave them tightly closed until morning.

Let your toddler climb in bed with you. For a new twist on a lazy Saturday morning, let your toddler snuggle between mommy and daddy for a half hour.

Get out and enjoy the sunrise. I'm telling you, I don't think I understood the lure of a gorgeous sunrise until I had kids. But now, I spend at least one morning a week on the patio with one of my kids, snuggling while the sun rises.

Get something done. I can pretty much guarantee there won't be a line at the checkout counter in the grocery store at 6:00 a.m. So beat the crowds and check some to-dos off your list with your toddler when you're both (sort of) wide-awake.

Do quiet time . . . toddler mom–style. Get out a stack of books or even a children's Bible and spend a half hour reading to your toddler, praying together, or even talking about Jesus. Okay, it won't exactly be quiet, but it'll be fun.

Moving to a Big-Kid Bed

I had to move Joey into a big-boy bed when he was about sixteen months old. This wasn't by choice—trust me: I loved the idea of him being trapped safely in Crib-catráz. But I had a little jailbreaker on my hands, and after the fourth time Joey pitched himself over the rails, I got motivated to find a better sleeping situation for him. Of course, *better* is a relative term. Because there are very few toddlers who possess the reasoning skills to stay in bed when mommy and daddy are downstairs, watching a movie on the couch.

Anyway, there will come a point when your toddler has the maturity and fortitude to make the switch to a big-kid bed. Or more likely, there may come a point when you're forced to move your still-immature toddler into a big-kid bed because you want to use the crib for a new baby or you no longer trust the crib to confine him. Either way, this is not something you can just do in one day. Unless, of course, you want to share your Ben & Jerry's with your kid every night, in which case you can just go onto Craigslist, buy a bed, and be done. But if you have lofty goals of, say, making sure your toddler stays in bed after you tuck him in for the entire night, then you may have to put some energy into it. Here are my suggestions.

Making the Big-Kid Bed Transition

Step one: Pick it up. Before you move your kid into a big-kid bed, you're going to have to actually beg, steal, or borrow a big-kid bed. Your first option is to pick up a toddler bed, which is like a cross between a twin bed and a white-water raft. Only it isn't waterproof. Toddler beds are handy because they are low to the ground, so if your kid does decide to dive out, he'll only fall about six inches. Your other choice is a regular twin bed, which is definitely the practical and frugal option (if you're one of those people) but is also a bit higher and a bit more daunting for a toddler.

Step two: Spruce it up. Once you have a bed, you're going to have to buy bedding. Let me warn you that your toddler's tastes are probably more "Lightning McQueen" or "Dora" than the retro-chic look you have in mind. And I can tell you from experience that once you start walking down the cartoon-character bedding path, it's a slippery slope that often ends up with you having a Disney Princess mini hide-a-bed in your living room. But if you want to go there, be my guest. Or you could just "surprise" your toddler with a supercute bedding set that you picked out.

Step three: Set it up. Spend some time making sure your kid's new big-kid bed is just perfect. Wash the sheets. Make the bed. Load it up with pillows and stuffed animals. Set some books on the bedside table. Make it look fun and nice and as if you've done something really special for him. If you have space, I recommend leaving your toddler's crib set up in his room (just scootch it to the side) for the first few weeks you're trying the big-kid bed. That way if your toddler has a really bad night, you have a backup plan so you can get some rest. If there's not room for both a crib and a bed in his room, keep a Pack 'n Play handy for emergencies.

Step four: Talk it up. This is where those acting classes you took in high school will pay off. Because you are going to convince your toddler that the big-kid bed is the most fun, most exciting, most special place that has ever existed. Hands down. Oh, and that puny crib over there? That's for babies. When Joey was making the transition, I set everything up when he was playing downstairs. Then I carried him into his room while covering his eyes and made the big reveal. We checked the bed out from headboard to footboard together, talking excitedly about every little piece. Climb into bed with your toddler, test it out, read a few books, and talk about how comfy, how great, and how fantastic the bed is.

Step five: Set the ground rules. Once you've talked it up, set some ground rules. Tell your kid how proud you are that he's ready to sleep in a big-kid bed. Explain how it's a special privilege to sleep in such a special bed, and you know he'll be able to show you he's a big kid. Then set your ground rules. In our house, the rule is that once mommy and daddy have tucked you in, you stay in bed until morning. And if you get up, it's straight to Crib-catráz.

Step six: Follow through. Most toddlers will pop right out of their beds just as soon as they realize there are no bars holding them in. It took Joey about twelve seconds. I hadn't even left the room. Now, this is probably going to make me sound like a hard-nosed stickler, but I'll just say it anyway:

The Christian Mama's Guide to Parenting a Toddler

don't let your kid get by with getting up out of his big-kid bed even once. Because the last thing you want is a two-year-old who thinks he can wander downstairs and get himself a string cheese at 2:00 a.m. It's better to just nip it in the bud. That first time that Joey hopped out of bed, I calmly told him that our rules were that if he got out of bed, he had to sleep in his crib. And I set him in his crib and gave him a kiss and left. And he screamed and cried and whined and moaned and threw a massive fit that made me want to go in there with a giant hot fudge sundae and apologize for making him so upset. But I didn't. I distracted myself with my own hot fudge sundae and stuck to my guns. The next night, it took him about three minutes to pop out of bed. The next, ten minutes. But after a few nights, he got the hint. And before long, he was sleeping in his big-kid bed with only the occasional backslide.

Getting Rid of Bedbugs

It's around the time that your kid makes the transition into a big-kid bed that the term "bedbug" will start to take on a whole new meaning. Your bed will literally become infested with small, snuggly little bedbugs that seem to think your bed is the one and only place to go when they're scared of monsters, need a drink, or have an itch. But as much as the idea of real bedbugs makes me shudder, I have to admit I kind of like bedbugs of the diaper-clad and dimpled variety. In fact, part of me smiles whenever one of my kids comes down and hops into bed between us. I pull that warm little bedbug up close to me and take a deep breath, savoring the sweet smell of my babies that are growing up too quickly.

But my nostalgia is often short-lived, because toddler-sized bedbugs may be cute, but they are also wiggly. And before long those sweet snuggles turn to tossing and turning and thrashing. I am forced to fumble around on my nightstand for a book to throw at my husband so he'll get up and carry said bedbugs back to their own beds.

I'm going to put on my responsible cap for a second and tell you that if you consistently but gently carry your kids back to their rooms before letting them snuggle in, you'll probably break the bedbug habit before it even starts. Another idea is to put a sleeping bag or quilt on the floor by your bed and let your kid sleep on the floor but not in your bed.

Okay now, I'm going to take my responsible cap off and put my mom cap on. Those bedbug-snuggling-next-to-you days are short. My six-year-old bedbug rarely comes down to my bed anymore. I kind of miss it. So, if you can handle the thrashing and the kicking, maybe ten minutes to snuggle isn't such a terrible thing.

8 Things You Can Do Now That You've Fought (and Won) the Bedtime Battle

There will be a day in ten years or so that you have to beg and plead with your kid to get out of bed before noon. I know that feels a bit ironic right now—you've spent months begging and pleading with God that your baby will just sleep through the night, and years training your toddler to stay in his big-kid bed—but that day will come. In the meantime, you can revel in the fact that you have at least met your very low expectations and taught your toddler to sleep (sometimes) and stay sleeping (most of the time). And to celebrate, here are some things you can do:

- Stay up late. (Yes, nine thirty totally counts as late.)
- Brag to your friends that your kid is a great sleeper. Who cares if they don't believe you?
- Brag to your mother-in-law that your kid is a great sleeper. She'll believe every word, so much so that she'll pass your words on verbatim to her quilting group.

The Christian Mama's Guide to Parenting a Toddler

- Know with confidence that your baby will be in bed before *Downton Abbey*. (You should probably still TiVo it, just in case.)
- Have sex with your husband. At night. In your bed.
- Make yourself a cup of coffee before your toddler gets up in the morning. No guarantees that you'll get to enjoy it alone, but at least you'll get to make it without someone swiping at the coffee beans.
- Stop wearing a bra to bed.
- Upgrade to a new video monitor—the kind where you can talk and your toddler can hear you. (Think: "Luke. This is your father. Now, get back in bed.")

SEVEN

Brainiacs on (Hot) Wheels

Learning and Growing with Your Toddler

By the time my kids were two (or something like that), they had each read John Piper's *Desiring God* (in Latin), and we're working on solving basic algebraic facts during their spare time. Or maybe I'm not remembering clearly. Either way, I know my kids were super smart. And, if your toddler isn't reading fluently and speaking conversational Mandarin by now, then intervention is surely in order. You need to head online *stat* and spend your life's savings on academic essentials like "Your Baby Can Solve the Quadratic Equation" CDs and upper-level Greek flash cards. You don't want your kid to fall behind, do you?

I'm totally kidding. (I bet you had no idea, did you?) But in all seriousness, the idea of academic readiness is such a hot topic with toddler parents these days. It's as if people are on a mission to make sure their kids are the smartest, most academically advanced two-year-olds in the history of the world. I'm sure their kids are brilliant, but I have to wonder if that's the most important thing to be focusing on.

I remember being at the park when Joey was a toddler and feeling pretty smug about the fact that my two-year-old had pointed to the blue slide and said, "Bu!" I looked around to see who had witnessed his brilliance and noticed another mom asking her daughter what color the slide was. "Azure," the genius-child said, clear as day. And her mom smiled at me and shrugged as if to say, "What can I do? The kid knows that there are many, many shades of blue and that slide is clearly not indigo or turquoise." Whatever. I left little Rainbow Bright to play with her mom and took Joey to the sandbox so he could eat some rocks.

A small part of me wanted to head right home and bust out the Crayola 64 and quiz my little brainiac—who, by the way, became quite adept at varying colors and still to this day calls his sister's light purple dress "primrose." But then I realized that the ability to name fifteen shades of blue is not an essential life skill. For anyone. And I'm just going to go out on a limb and say that all this academic pressure we're putting on our toddlers is really doing nothing to help their future success. Unless, of course, *azure* is a vocabulary word on the SAT.

I'm talking to you from the flip side now; I still have a toddler, but I also have two older kids who survived the academic pressure of toddlerhood. And—*shhhhh*; don't spread this around, or I may be shunned by the Toddler Intellectual Sisterhood—neither of my kids could identify their letters, much less read, when they were two. Neither of them was able to spout math facts or speak in another language or do anything of the sort. A major academic accomplishment was calling the slide "Bu!" or the teeter-totter "Geen!" And they're the smartest kids in the history of the earth. At least in my opinion.

My point is that toddler book knowledge—while handy when

it comes to impressing the other moms at the park—isn't all that important. I'm telling you this from experience, because by the time my older kids hit preschool, all those random facts we had painstakingly memorized were long forgotten. What was left was their curiosity about the world. Their inquisitiveness about how things work. Their love of learning. And their desire to know things. And these skills carried them much farther than knowing obscure vocabulary or how to perfectly dot their *i*'s and cross their *t*'s.

All that said, I want to use this chapter to tell you how to teach your kids to *learn* things, not *know* things. I'm not going to tell you how to teach your kids to read before they turn two (not that I would know how to do that anyway). I won't tell you how to teach geometry to a toddler or to help your kid's poetry skills emerge. Instead, I've put together several lists of ideas that will help your toddler learn to love learning. Because all that other stuff will come later, when your kid has a stronger grasp of language acquisition skills and can start learning Mandarin.

. . . .

Time-Out for Mom

For When You're Teaching Your Kid About God's World

"He made the earth by his power; he founded the world by his wisdom and stretched out the heavens by his understanding." (Jeremiah 51:15)

Heavenly Father, this world and everything in it were made by You. And I pray that as my kid explores this beautiful and wonderful world, he gains a sense of awe at the glory of Your creation. Help him never to lose his childlike faith and the amazement that comes from seeing the work of Your hand. Amen.

. . . .

Inspiring Future Scientists

One thing I can guarantee you've never heard a mom say: "Oh, I'd just love to inspire a love of the indoors for little Suzie!" Because if we're being honest, being inside isn't really all it's cracked up to be. I mean, I definitely see some benefits—namely, temperature control and lack of precipitation—but overall, I'm more inclined to be outdoors.

The good news for all you moms who are looking to inspire anything but a world-champion couch-sitter is that most toddlers are drawn to the out-of-doors. My son Will spends the majority of his inside time standing at the back door, pointing at our yard, and yelling, "Dat!" He loves getting out there, feeling the grass between his toes, the sand on his feet, the mud in his mouth. Okay, so we're working on that. And even though he eats the occasional slice of mud pie, some of our best times are spent outdoors, and yours can be too. Here are easy (and educational) ways to start teaching your toddler about God's world and to inspire a love of nature, science, and the environment for the future.

Ten Easy Ways to Teach Your Toddler About God's Creation
1. **Explore**. Go on a walk, and worry less about the destination than the journey. Stop to look at each leaf, each blade of grass, and each ant crawling along the sidewalk.
2. **Go stargazing**. Head outside at night with your toddler, and point out the stars and the moon. Or if it's the middle of the day, go cloud gazing; lie on the grass on a blanket and point out the fluffy clouds to your child.
3. **Plant a butterfly garden**. I'm no green thumb—I've killed four sets of flowers on my patio this summer alone. But a butterfly garden is an easy way to bring color into your yard or patio and to attract fun wildlife for your toddler to see. Just plant brightly colored flowers—marigolds, zinnias, hollyhocks—in small pots or in a plot. From there, the flowers will take over,

and before long, you'll have dozens of beautiful butterflies coming to visit.

4. **Become a photographer**. Head outside with your toddler and your camera, and ask your toddler to help you find beautiful and interesting things. Snap pictures, and then make a slideshow on your computer that you can look at together on a rainy day.

5. **Talk about the weather**. I love weather! And I'm absolutely—okay, *almost* absolutely—certain that when I walk up to someone and say, "How about this weather?" he or she is equally intrigued. Because things like heat waves and cold fronts and thunderstorms and snow flurries are super interesting. They're also tangible, which means your toddler can walk outside and actually feel cold or touch rain, turning weather into a fun educational activity. If you're feeling really brave, play outside together in the rain. Let your kid splash in a mud puddle or dance under a deluge. Yes, you'll have laundry to do later, but giving your kid the chance to get soaked is worth it.

6. **Play soccer**. Head outside with a soccer ball for an impromptu physics lesson. Try kicking the ball down a hill to see how fast it rolls. Then try the opposite and kick it up a hill. Next, try throwing the ball against a wall. It may seem like a game to you, but your toddler is learning about the laws of motion.

7. **Press flowers and leaves**. I read in a novel that women used to collect flowers and plants along the Oregon Trail and press them between the pages of books to dry. Later, they'd pull out the dried, preserved plants and remember their journey. We've done the same—not on the Oregon Trail, but on walks in our backyard or at my mom's house (where it's okay to pick flowers and leaves from plants). What a great tool to teach your toddler to notice the beauty in nature and to remember the journey they've been on.

8. **Play with ice**. Let your kid pour water into an ice cube tray and then find it frozen the next day. Then let your kid head outside and play with the ice while it turns back into water.

9. **Be magnetic**. Give your kid a magnet along with a handful of metal and nonmetal objects—a paper clip, a penny, a spoon, a plastic toy, a book. Let him see which things are attracted to the magnets and which aren't.

10. **Go to the pet store**. What's the difference between a dog and a fish? Seems like an easy question to you, but it may just stump your toddler who is still learning to evaluate the differences between things in the world. Head to the pet store and look at the various animals, and then discuss what you like best and least about each one.

Inspiring Great Readers

You have to promise that after I say this you won't come throw rotten tomatoes at my house, or something like that. I'm just reporting what I read on Mr. Google, so if you're going to throw rotten vegetables at anyone, it should probably be at your laptop. Here goes: lately, I've read article after article about those DVD programs that teach your baby to read before they are two. And these articles—written by expert educators and top universities—claim that such programs are not only ineffective, but they can also be damaging to a kid's future ability to learn. Babies' brains weren't wired to learn that way, and often babies who learn to memorize cues at a young age never learn how to actually decode words. Or understand context. If you don't believe me, ask Mr. Google yourself.

Now that I've dashed all your hopes of teaching your toddler to read before he reaches eighteen months, let me help you pick up the pieces: while babies' brains aren't wired to read when they're that young, they are certainly wired to learn. And that means you can lay the framework now to help your toddler become a great reader in the future by exposing him to literature in all sorts of creative ways. Here are ten ideas.

Ten Easy Ways to Teach Your Toddler to Love Reading

1. **Read. A lot**. The more your toddler is exposed to literature—even literature of the board-book sort—the more your toddler will love reading in the future.

2. **Visit the library**. Give your toddler a glimpse into the vast world of books—and give yourself a break from reading the same books over and over and over.

3. **Let your toddler play with his letters**. Pour a thin layer of cornmeal or flour into the bottom or a pie plate. Guide your toddler's hand as you "write" the letters in his name.

4. **Decorate with words**. You can pick up fancy-schmancy wooden letters at Pottery Barn Kids for about twelve dollars each, or go the DIY route and buy plain wooden letters at the craft store for about a dollar each and paint them yourself. Either way, hang the letters of your kid's name above his bedroom door. Or post the words *faith*, *hope*, and *love* on his wall. Or write the words to a nursery rhyme above the bed. The possibilities are endless—just like words.

5. **Make a big deal about letters**. When you see a *B* in a book, say, "Look, Benny, there's a *B*, just like in your name!" When you spot an *A* on a sign, squeal and say, "Wow! I just saw the first letter in the ABCs!"

6. **Try glow sticks**. Kids love glow sticks. Who am I kidding? *I* love glow sticks. And I love them even more now that I can pick up a fifteen-stick pack for a buck at Target. My favorite glow-stick activity is to activate the whole box and then turn out the lights and make letters and numbers on the floor with the sticks.

7. **Play with your kid's food**. Turn dinner into reading practice by arranging your kid's food into letters and words. Asparagus makes a great *A*, and two pieces of Canadian bacon stacked on top of each other make *B*. And if you want to start with an easy one, pretzel sticks, carrot sticks, and breadsticks are all dead ringers for *I*.

8. **Play with letters**. Sometimes information can just seep into your brain through osmosis. And while this rarely works for you when you're trying to remember where exactly you put your car keys, it certainly can work for your toddler when you expose him to letters over and over again. So pick up some toys that have letters on them—letter magnets, letter blocks, foam letter shapes—and just let him play.

9. **Make alphabet soup**. This works literally (like go buy a can of alphabet soup and serve it to your kid for lunch) and figuratively (toss some foam letters or letter magnets into a saucepan and give your kid a spoon and let him play while you're cooking dinner). Either way, your kid will have a lot of fun "eating" and learning about letters.

10. **Go cross-cultural**. Learn a few words in a foreign language and use them from time to time around the house.

Inspiring Future Mathematicians

Remember all that stuff I said about teach-your-baby-to-read programs? Well, same goes for math. It's a great idea to teach your toddler about quantity and numbers and counting, but creating laminated flash cards to help your toddler solve algebraic functions? Not so much. Still, you can be strategic—how's that for a math word?—about teaching your toddler about mathematical concepts without pushing him too far too soon.

Ten Easy Ways to Teach Your Toddler to Love Math

1. **Collect**. Go on a walk and let your kid collect things—rocks, leaves, shells—and then when you get home, sort them into groups. If your toddler knows how to count, see if he can tell you how many of each item he has.

2. **Play with beans**. I've already said this, but probably the best toy I ever bought for my kids was a ninety-nine-cent bag of

dry pinto beans. I pour the beans into a small bowl and then help my kids sort, count, make pictures, and even play with measuring cups and spoons. Just supervise young toddlers—dry beans are probably not the best thing to eat.

3. **Set the table**. Ask your toddler to set the table with one plate, one fork, one knife, and one cup for each person. Then go all Martha Stewart on him and ask him to go the double-fork route. Or the teacup and saucer route. (And yes, it may be a good idea to let your toddler practice with plastic plates and cups the first few times.)

4. **Play with money**. Dump out your kid's piggy bank and help him sort pennies, quarters, dimes, and nickels into piles.

5. **Sort laundry**. It may seem like doing laundry to you, but sorting socks into pairs or T-shirts by color is education to your toddler.

6. **Arrange your toys in rows**. Aside from really impressing Grandma, who is always on you to teach your kids to clean their rooms, when your toddler puts his trucks in a row, he's learning about quantity and mathematical organization.

7. **Mix apples and oranges**. Put your fruit bowl to good use and let your kid sort out apples from oranges. Once he gets better at counting, see if he can count how many of each you have.

8. **Play hide-and-seek with a twist**. Collect a basketful of small toys—stuffed animals, cars, dolls—and hide them around the house. Then have your toddler look for them, having him count how many items he has found.

9. **Bust out your bathroom scale**. Weigh several items—a shoe, a book, a gallon of milk—and then go on a walk around the house, trying to find heavy items (like a bucket or a clock) and light items (like the pillows on your couch).

10. **Take three steps forward**. Turn your backyard into a toddler Olympic challenge course. See if your toddler can take three steps forward and then two steps back. Then add some more difficult events, like the "triple jump," the "five-time

sidestep," and—my personal favorite—the "six-time boot scootin' boogie."

Inspiring Your Future Artist

When I think about exposing my kids to art and music, I think of three things: noise, paint, and glitter. And I think we can all agree that noise, paint, glitter, and toddlers don't mix. Because as much as most moms want to inspire their kids to be creative, most moms do not want to inspire their kids to be creatively messy. Or creatively noisy. But even uptight moms like me can learn to inspire future artists and musicians with some easy (and toddler-proof) activities that teach kids about rhythm, color, and design. Here are a few ideas.

Easy Ways to Expose Your Toddler to Music

1. **Make anything an instrument**. Pots can be banged, pans can be clanged, spoons can be jingled, and buckets can be drummed. Always look for ways to let your toddler make noise. (And, yes, it's totally fine for you to turn on your iPod and listen to Adele while you supervise your musician-in-the-making.)
2. **Dance like nobody is watching—even though somebody is**. When there's nobody in the room who's old enough to know that the Macarena went out of style in 1998, it'll give you the freedom to really let go and do the shimmy-shake. Just don't pull a muscle. Trust me: you don't even want to begin to explain why you were doing the Macarena on the dining room table to your doctor.
3. **Jingle bells**. String a few jingle bells onto small pieces of yarn and tie them around your toddler's ankles and wrists. And suddenly dancing, running, galloping, and walking become a musical feat.
4. **Go to a concert**. Google local musicians, and take your kid to a concert. Even if it's not kid's music, your toddler will love it.

5. **Make money cups**. Fill plastic cups with coins, and then cover with plastic wrap and let your little percussionist make some music.

6. **Clap patterns**. Clap three times and see if your toddler can repeat you. Then up the ante and clap four times with a little rapid beat in the middle, and see how she does.

7. **Learn your nursery rhymes**. I know it can be annoying to hear "wee-wee-wee all the way home" over and over and over. But all that over-and-over stuff is teaching your kid about rhyme and rhythm and meter and all sorts of other musical stuff that I don't understand . . . but I know it's important.

8. **Use scarves**. Last time I was at Goodwill, I noticed piles of big, bright scarves in all colors and sizes. I picked up several, went home, turned on some peppy music, and we played rhythmic gymnastics for hours. It was fun, and before long, my kids were all bopping to the beat. (Now, if only the Joe's Jeans section at Goodwill was as big as the colorful scarves section, I'd really be onto something.)

9. **Invest in CD songbooks**. I have tons of kids' CDs, but without a doubt, my kids have always been drawn toward music that has matching words and pictures. So, invest in a couple of CDs that have follow-along songbooks, and hand your toddler a book to follow along with in the car as you blast his favorite tunes.

10. **Sing old hymns**. It's amazing how much theology a kid can pick up through old hymns.

Ten Easy Ways to Encourage Your Budding Toddler Artist

1. **Make rainbow rice**. Put one cup of white rice (or, if you want, pasta), one tablespoon of rubbing alcohol, and a few drops of food coloring into a ziplock baggie. Repeat until you have three or four colors. Leave the bags open for a few hours to dry, and then pour into a plastic bin and let your kid play with the rainbow rice with tablespoons and measuring cups.

2. **Do high chair art**. Put a blob of applesauce or pudding on your kid's high chair tray, a heavy-duty bib on your kid, and let him finger "paint."

3. **Stamp with your food**. Sliced peppers, cucumbers, apples, and potatoes all make good stamps when dipped in paint. Just make sure your toddler is wearing an old T-shirt over his clothes because this activity can get messy. Oh, and make sure your kid knows that this is the one time you *don't* want him to eat his veggies.

4. **Make a tissue-paper masterpiece**. Tissue paper bleeds, which means if you get it wet with a spray bottle and clump it onto white paper, it will create a color-bleeding masterpiece. A color-bleeding masterpiece that even a toddler could do.

5. **Paint with marbles**. This is another one of those "only for moms who have nerves of steel around paint" projects. Basically, fill a disposable pie plate or lasagna pan with marbles. Then squirt some paint in and let your toddler wiggle the pan to make the marbles "paint" a picture.

6. **Whip up a batch of edible play dough**. My toddlers all ate play dough as if it were cookie dough the first time they touched it. So when Mr. Google showed me a recipe for edible play dough, I thought I had really hit the jackpot. And I had. Well, except for the fact that I ate more of it than my kids did. Still, just mix a cup of peanut butter with a cup of nonfat dry milk and add honey or agave nectar to taste. Then pop your toddler in his high chair and show him how to sculpt snakes, mountains, and towers. Oh, and how to indulge in peanut buttery comfort food, a skill that all kids should learn at a young age.

7. **Play with color**. Fill tall, see-through glasses with water or milk. Then drizzle in food coloring in various combinations and watch the liquid change color. Once you've mastered red, blue, and yellow, see if your toddler can guess how to make green or purple or neon turquoise.

8. **Make a discovery bottle.** I admit that when I first heard about this project, I immediately rejected it hands down because it involves messy dyes and glitter—two things I adamantly refuse to allow inside my house. But my sister, Alisa, promised me it would be okay (the caps get glued on), so I broke my own rules. And my rebellion worked—my toddler walked around holding his discovery bottle and shaking it for hours. Hand your toddler an empty plastic bottle and supervise as he fills it with fuzzy balls, small foam stickers, and large beads. Once he's done, add a few drops of food coloring or dye and a heap of glitter, and then fill the bottle with water. Screw the lid on—and this is the most important part—glue it shut with superglue. And there you have it: easy, safe, and (hopefully) mess-free toddler art.

9. **Make a ziplock swirl.** Place a colorful liquid—ketchup, mustard, hair gel, pudding—into a sturdy ziplock bag. Then squirt in another liquid of a contrasting color. Make sure the bag is sealed well; then let your toddler squish the bag to combine the colors.

10. **Let the glue begin!** Another thing I swore my kids would never be allowed to play with: glue. And another rule that I broke. Because (with careful supervision) even a young toddler can use glue, and use it correctly. Take out a piece of construction paper and several small objects—Cheerios, small dry pasta, or colorful buttons. Make several glue dots on the page with white glue and show your toddler how the glue will make the objects stick.

Academic Theory for Toddlers

I know this chapter is severely lacking in edu-speak. I never mentioned learning styles or Bloom's Taxonomy or any other key terms that would give you theoretical insight into your toddler's academic development. This isn't because I can't speak edu-speak—I used to be a teacher, and I currently work as a writer for an education company—so I can talk educational talk with the best of them. But in raising my own kids and reading countless articles on educational theory, I've come to the conclusion that it's more important for kids to learn to love learning than to learn random facts or skills. And while those other things will come (trust me: your kid will not escape kindergarten without learning his letters), they can come in time. For now, it's just fine to spend your time inspiring creativity, curiosity, inquisitiveness, and a love for God's creation.

EIGHT

Your Guide to Starting Preschool

Sending Your Toddler to School for the First Time

Sometime around when your toddler learns the words "no" and "mommy's new shoes" and "toilet water" (either separately or as part of the same sentence), you may suddenly get super-motivated to enroll your toddler in a preschool or Mom's Day Out program. Now, I want to make one thing clear right up front: preschool is not for your kid. It is for you. Sure, he may pick up a few neat tidbits about shapes or learn how to say, "A-A-A Apple" like a pro, but the main perk of preschool is that you get a few hours on your own.

Now, I have a feeling that some of the mamas reading this are the type of moms who want to spend every waking moment with their kids. That's great. And aside from being slightly suspicious that you might change your mind when your kid discovers Sharpies really do write on things that aren't paper, I'm also not afraid to go on record saying that it's really truly a great thing to be a 24/7 mommy. So, if you have the patience, energy, and stamina to dedicate 1,440 minutes of your undivided attention every day to your kid, then go for it.

I'm also not afraid to go on record saying I am not that kind of mom. I love spending time with my kids. But I also love having a few hours in the week when I don't have to worry about someone sticking my brand-new Toms in the toilet. And that's why I enrolled each of my kids in preschool.

Of course, there's a lot that goes into sending your kid to a preschool program. Like how do you choose a program? And how do you get into a program when the waiting list is 2.4 miles long and the top ten people on the list are related to the director? And once you're enrolled and ready, how do you make sure you make the most of your kid's valuable school time? And your precious time on your own?

. . . .

Time-Out for Mom

For When You're Sending Your Child off
Into the World for the First Time

"Being confident of this, that he who began a good work in you will carry it on to completion until the day of Christ Jesus." (Philippians 1:6)

Christ Jesus, thank You for my child. I am confident that You have begun a good work in his heart, and I pray that You carry it on as he enters the big, wide world. Lord, give him strength to resist temptation and a true desire to follow Your will. As my kid is away from me, remind him that he is never alone, because You are always standing beside him. Amen.

. . . .

The Christian Mama's Mini-Guide to Preschool

Choosing a Program

I have a 24-step process for choosing an educational program for kids. First, I set up a very complicated rubric that rates school systems based on educational prowess and student-to-teacher ratio. I then spreadsheet all that data and visit each school with a clipboard and observe each individual classroom to see how they follow biblical principles in and out of the classroom. Next, I do background checks on each of the teachers, double-checking the work that the school has probably already done just to make sure everything is up to my standards. Last, I use Google Maps to assess driving-distance scenarios in all types of traffic to make sure I can adequately manage preschool drop-off on busy mornings.

Um, I'm lying. (You probably already knew that, since I've made it clear that spreadsheets and I just don't get along.) Honestly, I chose Joey's preschool based on two factors: (1) my friends' recommendations, and (2) whether the programs my friends recommended had space on their waiting list. And that system worked for me. Joey got into a fantastic preschool program that we both loved—one I have continued to send my kids to for six years now.

All the stress over ratings and spreadsheets and academic prowess may seem important when choosing a school, but if I'm being honest, none of that stuff matters. Because you're dealing with a toddler. A toddler who will thrive in any school where he is surrounded by teachers who love kids and love Jesus. And as long as you find a school that has a good, strong biblical foundation and that hires teachers who clearly love your kid, you're set. No, you're more than set. You're ready to go to the coffee shop for a genuine, bona fide stay-at-home mom break.

Getting "School" Supplies

There's an added bonus to enrolling your kid in preschool: you get to go shopping. Now, I know to some of you, the idea of dragging your toddler into Target to pick out backpacks and lunch boxes sounds like torture, in which case you can go the boring, quick, and efficient route and place an order on Amazon. But if you're anything like me, the idea of browsing Bob the Builder backpacks while bribing your toddler to sit still in the cart by feeding him animal crackers sounds like a lot of fun. And if you're up for that, then I say make a mommy-and-me day out of it and add a fun lunch out at McDonald's and a stop-off at the bookstore to add some back-to-school books to the deal. We're making memories here, people.

I'm actually totally serious—I love back-to-school shopping—crowded stores, cranky toddlers, and all. And when I enrolled my son in preschool, the idea of taking him shopping to get a cute little toddler backpack and a sports-themed nap mat pretty much made my week. (Okay, so I didn't have a lot going on back then.) We went all over town finding the best preschool gear we could. And I failed miserably. I know what you're thinking: *How can you fail at buying a backpack and a nap mat?* Let me just tell you . . .

Toddler School Supply Failures to Avoid

Failure #1: Buying too small. You know those cute little toddler backpacks that look oh-so-adorable on your kid's back? Well, turns out they are more adorable than functional. And after trying every possible way to fit both his water bottle and his lunch box in said backpack, I learned that neither item fit. Which meant Joey went to school every day with an empty, albeit cute, backpack, while I carried his lunch. I suggest buying a regular-sized backpack that will fit his lunch, his extra clothes, and his art projects. I know it probably looks ginormous on his back, but let me just let you in on a little secret: your toddler's probably not going to carry that backpack farther than twenty feet anyway. And once you have to pick it up, you'll thank me that you aren't already lugging around his lunch box and (wet) painted picture.

Failure #2: Buying a lunch box that doesn't fit your style. Have you seen those cute little bento-style lunches that moms (moms who exist only on the pages of parenting magazines, by the way) make for their kids? I love them! Or at least I thought I loved them. So last year before school, I bought these really cool bento-style lunch boxes for my kids so that I, too, could send my kids' eggs decorated like chickens and cute little ham-piglets in their lunch. But then school started. And—this might come as a shock to you—I never once made a bento box for my kids. I made lots of peanut butter sandwiches, but never once did I create any food item that resembled an animal or flower. And therefore, those cute (and expensive) bento boxes stayed on the shelf. There are tons of lunch boxes out there, and I just urge you to consider the type of food you will be packing before investing in one.

Failure #3: Skimping on the nap mat. When I noticed that Joey's supply list called for a nap mat, I asked Mr. Google to find me one and discovered that the cheapest ones were, like, thirty-five dollars! That's *seven* Mocha Coconut Frappuccinos, in case you don't feel like doing the math. Sure, they had cute (attached) pillows and handy (attached) straps, but I still couldn't stomach the thought of coughing up that much cash for a nap mat. So, I jerry-rigged a nap mat out of his old sleeping bag, a belt, and a doll pillow. And what seemed like a brilliant idea at the time soon became the bane of my existence as I spent countless treks into the school carrying an unrolled sleeping bag while balancing a doll pillow in one hand and a belt in the other. It wasn't even September before I decided that a few frappucinos was a small price to pay for the convenience of a mat that actually stayed rolled.

Failure #4: Buying cute shoes. Hi, my name is Erin, and I have a (major) kid shoe addiction. I couldn't care less about my own shoes—a pair of Toms and some flip-flops is all I need. But my daughter? Well, let's just say she has these cute hot pink knee-high boots that I got her for Valentine's Day that have little rhinestone hearts on the side. And Oh. My. Goodness. I could just swoon every time I see her in them. Anyway, as you can imagine, she has adorable shoes to go with every adorable outfit. But I learned fairly quickly that the school's policy that "kids should wear tennis shoes" is in place for a reason. Because technically it's kind of hard for kids to run around the playground wearing strappy sandals—and even harder for teachers to police the Tempra paint splatters around your kid's fancy shoes. It's best to just buy a sturdy, inexpensive pair of Velcro sneakers and save the zebra-striped boots for church days.

Packing Your Kid's Lunch

On Joey's first day of preschool, I carefully packed his lunch and then wrote a little note to his teacher, warning her that "Joey tends to put too much food in his mouth at the same time, so could you please watch him closely to make sure he doesn't choke?" Don't laugh. You know you've at least considered doing the same thing. Toddlers are notoriously bad eaters! Not bad as in they don't eat, but bad as in they take huge bites, jam food into their mouths, run while eating, and smear yogurt through their hair. It's not pretty. And I can only imagine the scene when there are ten toddlers eating around the same table. It's enough to make any toddler mama start to worry.

The trick to packing a no-worry toddler lunch is to pack food that's easy for your toddler to eat on his own. Which pretty much means finger foods that your toddler can easily pick up by himself. And sadly, that means yogurt (too messy), soup (too liquidy), and pudding (too sugary, messy, and liquidy) are out. But since I'm always here to help you out, I've put together a list of foods that are "in." Here are my best toddler lunch ideas.

Ten Easy, Healthy, and Packable Toddler Lunch Ideas

1. **Pasta salad**. Most kids I know love pasta. And cold pasta is no exception. Toss some leftover whole wheat pasta with small chunks of ham, turkey, cheese, and veggies for an easy and toddler-friendly lunch.

2. **Antipasto plate**. My mother-in-law came to visit a few months ago and asked my kids what they wanted for lunch, and they replied with "antipasti." What else? At our house, we use the word "antipasti plate" for a plateful of whatever random cheeses, meats, crackers, and veggies we have in the fridge. Just grab a Tupperware container—or that bento box you bought for back-to-school—and fill it with small chunks of cheese and meat, a few peas, cucumbers, or cut tomatoes. Throw some whole wheat crackers into your kid's lunch box, and you're set.

3. **Frozen veggies**. Toss a small container with frozen peas or corn into your kid's lunch. The veggies will not only keep everything else cool but will also defrost by lunchtime for an easy and healthy snack.

4. **Burrito pinwheels**. Spread refried beans on a whole wheat tortilla and sprinkle with cheese. Roll it up and slice it into pinwheels that are not only easy to pick up, but also delicious. If the grated cheese falls out, heat it to melt the cheese, and then wrap it in tinfoil, and it will still be a little warm when your kid eats it. You can also make tortilla pinwheels with deli meat and cheese or even peanut butter.

5. **Sandwich cutouts**. This works for toddlers, big kids, and

adults alike. Make a sandwich—any kind of sandwich—and use cookie cutters to cut it into fun shapes. At Christmas, make a Christmas tree. In the spring, a flower. Oh, and on national Rectangle Day, a rectangle.

6. **Muffins**. Muffins have gotten a bad rap lately—probably because the ones you can buy at the coffee shop are pretty much cupcakes with sugar on top. But there are lots of healthy muffin recipes that are chock-full of veggies and even protein that you can make for your kids. Make a double batch of flax, ham, and cheese muffins or zucchini-pumpkin muffins, and then freeze the leftovers and pop one or two in your toddler's lunch box.

7. **Hummus**. I actually think it's kind of bizarre that my kids like hummus as much as they do. It is, after all, smooshed-up chickpeas. But my kids seem to look past hummus's humble legume roots and love it for its creamy deliciousness. They'll pretty much eat anything as long as it's smothered in the stuff. Pack thinly sliced bell peppers or cucumbers along with hummus for dipping, and your kid will chow down.

8. **Cheese crisps**. When my friend Sarah told me she made her own cheese crackers, my gut reaction was to dismiss her as an overachiever mom and head to the grocery store for some Cheese-Its. But then she told me how she did it—literally, she sticks a small pile of shredded parmesan, cheddar, or jack cheese on a nonstick cookie sheet and bakes her crisps until they're crunchy—and I decided she's a genius.

9. **Chicken salad**. I know chicken salad sounds totally adult-ish (and totally un-toddlerish) but it's actually a great way to pack healthy protein in a way that your toddler will eat it. Chop up leftover chicken and mix with a little bit of mayo as well as chopped-up grapes, strawberries, or pineapple. Pack along an ice pack to keep it cold and some pita bread cut into triangles for dipping and you have an easy and healthy lunch.

10. **Breakfast for lunch**. Make a fun play on breakfast-for-dinner

and pack breakfast-for-lunch. Pack dry cereal along with a sippy cup full of milk—which, by the way has the same nutrition eaten separately as it does together. Or slice up a hard-boiled egg and pack it with some ham slices and an English muffin. Even leftover pancakes, waffles, or French toast sliced into strips can make a fun toddler lunch.

Dropping Your Baby off at School

When Joey's first day of preschool dawned, I woke him up early. I dressed him in his cutest (which meant least stained) clothes and packed his brand-new monkey lunch box with healthy (and adequately chopped) food. He was ready. But I wasn't. As badly—make that desperately—as I needed the break, the idea of sending my baby off to school made me melt into a puddle of mommy guilt. What if he missed me? What if he needed his mommy? What if he noticed I was leaving him in a strange place and freaked out that I was abandoning him and then spent the whole day sobbing at the door for me to come back?

When we got to the school, I bravely made the walk into the building, went to his classroom, and loaded his gear into his cubby. I braced myself for the crying meltdown I was sure would ensue and gave him a little pep talk about how mommy was only going to be gone for a little bit, and his teachers would be there to help him. He shrugged, gave me a hug, and then walked into the classroom and started playing with trucks. And he didn't shed a tear. He didn't even give me the courtesy of a longing glance back at the door. I'm not even sure he noticed I left.

I, of course, went out into the car and sat in the driver's seat with tears streaming down my face, blubbering about my poor *bay-bee!* My poor, sweet *bay-bee* whom I had left all alone in that big, daunting classroom with the rainbow-covered walls and novel toys that he just loved to play with. How could I have done that to him?

So, three excruciating hours later, I picked him up. The teachers reported that he played happily the whole time, hadn't cried at all, and had even made a few friends. Of course, they must have been exaggerating a little—surely he cried for me once, didn't he?—but it was a bit reassuring to know that he enjoyed his time. And after a few more car-blubbering incidents, I started to enjoy my time as well. Of course, not all kids handle the drop-off as well as Joey did. My daughter, Kate, sobbed hysterically for over an hour the first time I sent her to preschool. Poor baby! Here are some tips on how to make the drop-off transition easier (notice I said easier, not easy.)

Tips for Making Drop-off Easier

1. **Leave quickly.** I know your instinct is to hover outside the door, listening to make sure your kid settles down. But stealthy as you are, chances are good your kid will spot you. Or smell you. Either way, your best bet is to head home and let the teacher soothe your child. Or at the very least, go out to the parking lot and wait in your car, where there will be no chance of an accidental mom-spotting.

2. **Pre-coach your kid.** Prep your kid for drop-off ahead of time. A simple explanation that assures your kid that (a) he'll be doing fun things, and (b) you'll be coming back can work wonders for separation anxiety. Both yours and his.

3. **Resist the temptation to go into the classroom** to soothe your kid unless there is a true emergency. Because as much as you want to go in there and snuggle that little guy, all that's going to say to him is that if he cries long enough and hard enough, you'll come back sooner.

4. **Send a lovey with your kid.** My friend Mary picked up two little friendship bracelets. As she walks into preschool each day, Mary slips one on her daughter's wrist and the other on her own wrist. Their shared bracelets are a reminder to each of them that they will be together soon. How's that for adorable?

Behavior at School

You may think bad behavior at school will never happen to you. I know I did. I assumed my teacher's pet attitude and the fact that I wouldn't have dared cause an interruption to the learning environment at school had been passed on to my kids. (If you're one of my old teachers and you're reading this, hi! I'm sure you remember this exactly as I do, right?) Therefore, I assumed my kids would be on their best behavior at preschool.

And I assumed wrong. With my son Joey—well, let's just say I got very used to hearing about "accidental" pushing and "I forgot to share" incidents. Those "accidents" coupled with taking a wild, boisterous two-year-old boy and putting him in a classroom with sweet-as-pie girls, led to a good number of after-school conversations with his very patient (and very forgiving) teachers.

I'm not saying this to pick on little boys, either, because my people-pleaser daughter—the kid I swore would never, ever have trouble with anyone—has even had the occasional school issue as well. With her, they are rare. I can count on one hand the number of times a teacher gave a less-than-glowing report in five years of school, but there certainly have been times when her teacher looked me in the eye and said she'd had a rough day.

Your kid will misbehave at school at some time. It's just going to happen. And while it's not okay—I can't even imagine how hard it is on teachers to deal with toddler misbehavior on top of toddler crafts and toddler tears—it is normal. And it's part of your toddler's growing and learning process. That said, *you* have to know how to deal with it so you can be the supermom who does everything right when it happens. So I asked my mom—the one who has more than thirty-five years working as an educator in schools and knows her stuff when it comes to school misbehavior—for her best tips.

Tips for Dealing with School Misbehavior

1. Let the teacher deal with it. This is so hard for me because I want to swoop in and make everything all right. But my mom reminded me that teachers are trained to deal with little toddler misbehaviors. And while it's great that they are communicating with you, they're probably not telling you about the misbehavior because they expect you to dole out additional consequences when you get home. Remember that whatever happened, happened at school. And therefore, the teacher dealt with it in a school-appropriate way. And that means that unless we're talking about a very serious behavior issue, you can probably skip the time-out when you get home.

2. **Practice the positive**. Once you've discussed how sad you were about what happened, it's probably better to drop the lecture (trust me: even a two-year-old gets tired of nagging). Instead, spend the next couple of days re-teaching your kid the positive. If it was a sharing issue, sit down with your kid and practice good sharing together. If it was a hitting issue, practice positive ways to respond to angry feelings. This is especially important right before the next school day so your kid can walk into the classroom ready to do the right thing.

3. **Resist the urge to talk, talk, talk**. This goes hand in hand with #2—your kid simply isn't going to learn character through a lecture. And that's why it's really important to know the difference between talking and teaching. Talking is telling them what they shouldn't do. Teaching is talking to them about what they should do. So spend time having meaningful conversations, asking questions, and listening carefully for clues as to what your child is thinking and feeling; then frame growth statements through their responses. Say, "What do you think you could do differently?" or "How are you going to be kind to your friends tomorrow?" This will allow your toddler to learn from a young age how to make positive choices because he wants to, not because you told him to.

4. **Don't take it personally**. Your kid is not a reflection of you. Let me repeat that: your kid's behavior is not a reflection of

your behavior. And that means when your kid makes bad choices, your job is to help your kid learn and grow, not to chastise yourself for your parenting downfalls.

5. **Don't be afraid to intervene in a big way.** My mom says that most toddler behavior issues are just that—minor toddler behavior issues. Chalk them up as minor blips as kids learn about socialization and school and move on. But my mom said that she occasionally sees a kid that just isn't functioning well in school—and the hitting, biting, pushing, screaming, or crying just gets worse and worse. If this is the case with your kid, it's important that you intervene right away. Call a meeting with the teacher or the headmaster, express your concerns and find out what you need to do to assure your kid's success in preschool.

Making the Most of Your Mom Time

This probably goes without saying, but those three hours between preschool drop-off and preschool pickup are yours. Like, yours alone. And since I'm guessing you've probably become quite accustomed to not having any time to yourself, it may take you a while to get used to it. But I'm sure you'll figure it out.

Just in case you're a bit slow to catch on (I get it: long-standing habits are hard to break), let me conclude this chapter by giving you a few ideas of what you can do to occupy this time. I bet in a few weeks, you'll be able to even take a few steps on your own and—gasp!—make plans to lunch with your mom. You go, girl!

Ten Things You Can Do When Your Kid Is in Preschool

1. **Do a Bible study or devotional.** Not only will you be able to focus and pray when your house is quiet and there aren't any toddlers around to tear the pages in your Bible, but spending some alone time with God can work wonders for your frazzled soul.

2. **Exercise.** Go on a jog without pushing a heavy jogging stroller or sign up for Dancercise at the gym without worrying about being called out of class to deal with a mishap in the toddler playroom.

3. **Have coffee with a friend.** This works best if your friend's kids are also in preschool, but even if she brings her kids along, at least it's not your kid who is spilling hot cocoa all over the floor.

4. **Build the best Pinterest board known to Pinterest.** Every recipe you want to (someday) cook and every craft you want to (someday) do can be in one handy place.

5. **Actually do one of the crafts (or make one of the recipes) on your Pinterest board.** Finally, you actually have time to make that crocheted blanket or papier-mâché tissue holder you've been drooling over.

6. **Visit your husband at work.** Drop by your hubby's office with a latte and a kiss.

7. **Clean your house.** My friend Rebecca reserves one day of preschool every week for housecleaning. Now, that may be going a bit too far by my standards (cleaning *every* week?), but with an occasional touch-up, your house will probably be neater than it's been, well, since your kid was born.

8. **Plan dinner.** With all this free time you have, you can not only go to the grocery store without worrying about anyone throwing cans at passers-by, but you could actually plan a week's—heck, a month's—dinners that you could prep ahead to avoid the crazy dinnertime rush.

9. **Do laundry.** You know that machine that's next to your washer? Turns out it was created to dry clothes, not to store them. You can actually take the clothes out, fold them, and put them in drawers, and then—get this—actually find things to wear instead of digging through the dryer and screaming about the sock monster.

10. **Get a pedicure.** Hey, even if you can't afford to go to the

spa and get a real, live pedicure, slapping on some nail polish and actually waiting for it to dry before running around outside will be a vast improvement from the pedis you've had recently. So treat yourself!

NINE

"I've Never Seen This Before"

And Other Things You'd Prefer Not to Hear from Your Pediatrician

have a very important reminder from you, courtesy of my friend Joanne: you need to protect your toddler from the dangers of carrots. Joanne learned this very important lesson after she decided it would be a good mom thing to do if she stocked her fridge with already-washed, already peeled carrots so her toddler son, David, would be motivated to eat his veggies. The first time her little Bugs Bunny asked for a carrot, she proudly told him from her perch on the couch that he could grab one all by himself. Bravo, smart and savvy mom!

Of course, even the best-laid plans get derailed when there's a toddler involved. And in the case of David's carrot fix, that involved him deciding that mommy definitely wouldn't want him to use a knife to cut the carrot (good thinking, David) and therefore he could probably break the carrot tip off with his thumb. Which resulted in a frantic trip to the emergency room, where the ER doctor said those five words that haunt every toddler mommy: "I've *never* seen this before." David had gotten a shard of carrot stuck between his fingernail and the nail bed. And Joanne learned an important lesson about the perils of vegetables.

Life with a toddler is—well, let's just call it interesting. Just when you start thinking you don't really need to spend $16.95 on cabinet locks because there is no way your toddler is tall enough to reach the high cabinets, you learn that height is no match for a toddler's motivation. And just when you start thinking your house is certainly baby-proofed enough for you to run to the kitchen to grab yourself a cup of coffee, you learn that *baby-proof* is a relative term. A relative term that clearly does not account for the fact that your kid would rather play the piano while standing and balancing precariously on the keys than play it with his fingers.

Yes, just when you finally got the green light to stop heading to the pediatrician's office for well checks every three months, you suddenly find yourself going to the pediatrician's office for other reasons. And these reasons involve more, um, complicated things . . . like carrot shards. In this chapter, I'm going to try to help you figure out how to avoid "I've never seen this before" situations while simultaneously knowing what to do when the inevitable happens.

Preventing "I've Never Seen This Before" Incidents

I've told you before that I'm a big rule follower. So you'd better believe that the day Joey learned to crawl, I heeded Mr. Google's well-meaning but totally misguided advice and baby-proofed my house. I'm not one for extremes, so I skipped the jumbo foam stairwell protector (Buy Buy Baby was out), but I did manage to buy just about every other babyproofing item on the market. By the time my husband got home from work, the coffee table was surrounded by a thick, gray foam barrier, the hearth had a massive plastic-and-foam fence surrounding it, and the cabinets could only be opened and closed using a small magnet doodad.

I took a step back, assessed everything, and then smiled the smile of one who knows: I had thought of everything. There was no way that baby of mine was going to get hurt at my house. And I was right. When Joey was a baby, he never once got hurt. Of course, when Joey was a baby, he was too inexperienced in the laws of human movement to understand that the fastest way off the couch is to climb onto the back and then swing down to the floor via the floor lamp.

The word *baby-proofing* is a misnomer, because by and large, babies are fairly immobile. They can get themselves into trouble—don't get me wrong—but the amount of damage a baby can cause is negligible compared to the sheer magnitude of destruction a toddler can inflict. And while you may think you've managed to successfully baby-proof your house, you may want to give your house (and your life) a once-over before your baby gets too far into toddlerhood. Because toddler-proofing? Well, that's a whole different ball game, my friends.

Just to give you a glimpse into what you're up against, here are a few of the places and situations where your toddler and you may not see eye-to-eye safety-wise:

You think: *The dishwasher needs loading.*

Your toddler thinks: *Mom's about to play in that fun toy box where she stores all sorts of fun and shiny, albeit sharp, toys. I'd better go play with her.*

You think: *Balloons! I loved balloons when I was a kid.*

Your toddler thinks: *Mom just got me another one of those big, chewy lollipops that tastes funny. Maybe I just need to chew through this gummy rubber layer to reach a cream-filled center.*

You think: *I'm sure I can leave this soup boiling while I run to the bathroom real quick.*

Your toddler thinks: *My soup?! Did she forget about my soup?! Hello! I'd better go check to make sure it's not burning while she's gone.*

You think: *Crisis! I forgot to bring toys to my mother-in-law's dinner party. Let me just screw the diaper rash cream lid on super tight and he can play with that. Crisis averted.*

Your toddler thinks: *"Frosting" on the wall, "frosting" on the couch, "frosting" on the carpet, "frosting" in my mouth . . .*

You think: *The dog just loves Junior so much! Good boy, Rover!*

Your toddler thinks: *The dog just loves me so much! I'd better go pull his tail and poke his eyes a bit just to remind him of our undying mutual affection.*

You think: *This lavender-scented baby lotion would smell so yummy on those teeny-tiny toes.*

Your toddler thinks: *Smoothie!*

You think: *Let me just set my purse down and I'll head out and unload the groceries.*

Your toddler thinks: *Mom's been holding out on me. This is a treasure trove! Nail scissors, gum, a Sharpie, and this fun, shaky bottle full of tiny, green pellets. Score!*

. . . .

Time-Out for Mom

For When You're Praying for Your Kid's Safety

"Do not be anxious about anything, but in every situation, by prayer

and petition, with thanksgiving, present your requests to God."
(Philippians 4:6)

Lord God, You are my kid's ultimate protector. You have covered him with the might of Your love and with the strength of Your angels. I pray that You stay near to him, keeping him safe from physical harm, but also from emotional and spiritual harm. Lord, relieve me of any anxiety I have over my kid's health and safety. I know that You are ultimately in control, and I trust my baby to Your all-knowing and all-loving hands. Amen.

. . . .

Toddler-Proofing Your Life

Okay, I know I'm joking about something that's not funny at all. Toddler safety isn't a laughing matter. There is nothing worse than watching a little one get hurt—especially for a mom who can not only feel her kid's pain acutely but also feels a (guilty) sense of responsibility anytime something bad happens. So, even if you baby-proofed à la me, you still need to expect the unexpected and be prepared. And to help you out, I've come up with a list of ways you can toddler-proof your life:

Step 1: Try to Get into Your Toddler's Mind

Get down on your hands and knees and assess your house from your toddler's viewpoint. That drapery cord hanging down? It looks like a long, swinging licorice stick to your kid. The table and chairs? Yes, it's a jungle gym. Once you've assessed your house from down low, do your best to come up with safe toddler solutions for each safety hazard.

Step 2: Teach and Re-teach

I don't have to tell you that your kid is a regular smarty-pants, but I might have to tell you that all that brainpower is being wasted if you don't give your kid the chance to use it. Young toddlers—yes, even your wild and crazy one-year-old—can understand that certain things are off-limits. Explain to your toddler that the fireplace can cause an *owie* or the stairs can be a boo-boo if he falls down them. Even if he doesn't remember the first ten times you explain it, eventually he'll figure out that mommy really (*really*) doesn't want him going up the stairs on his own.

Step 3: Put Your Stuff Away

Get your toys—I mean, your stuff—off the floor. That means your shoes, your purse, your iPhone, and your coffee mug should all be put away in a safe, out-of-reach spot. And while I'm turning into my mother, you may want to consider coming up with an organizational system for all that mail too. The less stuff that's strewn about, the less stuff your baby will be able to trip over. Or stuff into his ear canal.

Step 4: Get Rid of Stuff You Don't Need

Now, I'm not trying to get all Simply Organized on you and tell you that you should minimize in order to avoid safety hazards, but if I'm being 100 percent honest, you should probably minimize in order to avoid safety hazards. After all, every knickknack that heads off to Goodwill is one more knickknack your kid won't try to eat.

Step 5: Look at Your Kitchen as a Danger Zone

Hot fire, sharp knives, caustic chemicals, boiling water. The dangers your toddler can encounter in your kitchen can rival the scariest episode of *Wipeout*—only without the protective measures they take to ensure safety on TV. One thing I've done is leave one cabinet un-childproofed. I've filled that cabinet with toddler-proof kitchen implements, like plastic colanders, measuring cups, and rubber spatulas. That way, when I'm cooking dinner, my kids have a place where they can play safely, and I don't have to worry about them getting into the cleaning supplies.

Step 6: Watch the Water

Behind the kitchen, the bathroom is the next scariest place for toddlers (and not only because toddlers have a penchant for putting things in the toilet). Keep your bathroom doors shut—and whenever your kid is near water, watch him closely. I also suggest getting some sort of a protective lock for the toilet lid, getting a spout cover for the bath faucet, and turning your hot water heater down to below 120 degrees to prevent burns should your toddler accidentally turn on the water.

Step 7: Lock up the Meds

I started to tell you to keep your medicines on the tip-top shelf of your medicine cabinet, and then I remembered that it wasn't two weeks ago that I watched my one-year-old climb onto the bathroom counter by making a set of stairs with the drawers. Luckily, I watched him do it and was able to prevent a medicine mishap, but it's always better to be safe than sorry when it comes to medications. Lock them up in a medicine safe and put the safe on the highest shelf of your medicine cabinet. Oh, and put the key somewhere out of reach too.

Step 8: Lock up Your Makeup and Lotions Too

My latest call to the poison control center was when Will decided to drink a makeup smoothie. I watched the whole thing unfold, and I'm still in awe of the speed and dexterity he showed as he pulled the cap off the foundation and glugged down the entire bottle in the time it took me to put on mascara. It turns out that all makeup is nontoxic (good to know), so Will was fine, but it did take me a good ten minutes to wipe all the "long-lasting formula" out from between his teeth. And my makeup has now been moved to the top shelf in the bathroom cabinet.

Step 9: Buy a Baby Gate . . . or Six

I know you want to let your toddler roam free, to explore and learn and get the most out of his world. That's great. But may I suggest that you make that world a bit smaller? Because trust me; your life will be a whole lot easier if you have a strong toddler-proof gate at the top of the stairs.

Step 10: Be Doubly—No, Triply—Diligent

I've diligently assessed my house for safety hazards—several times—but since I never in my wildest dreams would've guessed that my fourteen-month-old Will would even consider climbing on top of his Cozy Coupe and onto the mantel, I didn't think to move the Cozy Coupe away from the mantel. Even if you think you've thought of everything, you still need to be diligent to keep an eye on your toddler. Which means—hard as it is—Facebook may have to wait until your kid takes a nap or heads off to first grade.

Preventing Toddler Illness

About halfway through last winter's seemingly endless cold season, I called my pediatrician because I was concerned that my youngest, Will, had something seriously wrong with him. Germs seemed to really have taken a liking to him, and my poor baby had faced cold after flu after stomach bug for nearly the entire winter. My pediatrician calmly reassured me that Will certainly did have something wrong with him: it's called *thirdkiditis.* And kids with thirdkiditis have the unfortunate problem of being exposed to each and every germ that hitches a ride home with their older siblings. Poor babies!

But even kids with secondkiditis and firstkiditis get sick a lot. Toddlers not only have immature immune systems, but they also have an uncanny knack for eating germ-ridden objects and wiping bodily fluids in places where bodily fluids don't belong. And while I don't want to minimize how horrible it is when your kid gets sick— it's incredibly sad to watch a little one suffer—I also want to point out that childhood colds and flus are a part of life. And the vast majority of the time, with a little Mama TLC and some rest, your kid will be just fine.

Of course, the best-case scenario is that your kid doesn't get sick in the first place. It may seem like an uphill battle to try to fight germs when your kid insists on drinking out of the drinking fountain drain (as my daughter explained: the water in the bottom of the fountain is "warmer" and therefore "more delicious"), there are things you can do to help your toddler stay healthy. Since I'm not an immunologist (or even a nurse), I decided to ask my RN friend Jordyn Redwood to give me her best tips for keeping toddlers germ free (or at least more germ free than they would be otherwise). Here's her advice:

Eight Nurse-Approved Tips to Keep Your Toddler Healthy

1. **Make sure your kid's shots are up-to-date**. I know that my just saying that makes some of you very, very irritated. I'm sorry. But as much as I'd like to remain neutral on this hot-button issue, I can't find a single doctor or nurse who will endorse my writing if I don't tell you how important it is for your toddler to get vaccinated. I know you've heard horror stories about immunizations (I admit that I've had my share of paranoid moments when I've considered skipping out on shots), and I know it's heart wrenching to watch your baby being pricked by needle after needle, but your child's health, your community's health, and our country's health depend on it. So before you decide for or against immunizations, have a serious, heartfelt discussion with your pediatrician about the risks and benefits.

2. **Teach hand washing at an early age**. I was in a disgusting public bathroom a few weeks ago when a little girl (maybe six years old) walked out of the stall and proudly announced to her mom that she didn't need to wash her hands because she "didn't touch anything while she went pee." Uh-huh. Start teaching your toddler now to wash his

hands after using the toilet, after petting animals, after playing outside, and before mealtime, so it becomes a habit. A habit that is well-established before he is old enough to argue.

3. **Eat food, not germs**. Remind your toddler (often) that food is for eating. Which means that toys, rocks, leaves, and that sticky piece of already-chewed gum on the sidewalk are *not* for eating. When your kid does mistakenly think that the bathroom door handle is a lollipop, immediately pull him away. But don't make a big deal of it. I know a few toddlers— I won't name names—who seem to think mommy dramatics mean they should do something more, not less.

4. **Eat healthy food**. Up your kid's germ-fighting power by providing loads of healthy fruits and vegetables in his diet. And since we're talking about eating healthy, adding some extra produce into your diet to boost your own immunity can't hurt either. After all, germ catching can often be a family affair.

5. **Drink plenty of water**. Healthy kids are less likely to get sick—and a big part of staying healthy is staying hydrated. So make sure your kid drinks plenty of water.

6. **Get some sleep**. It's common sense that a well-rested, well-fed kid has more germ-fighting power. So make sure your kid is getting enough sleep. (And that goes for you, too, missy. You can always TiVo *Parks and Recreation* and watch it tomorrow during nap time.)

7. **Limit your kid's exposure to germs**. I know this is easier said than done, but do your best to keep your toddler away from sick kids. That means no cousin playtime when you know your nephew has strep, and no neighborly visits when you know your neighbor's kids are getting over a cold. Of course, the flip side to this means you're going to have to keep your kid home and away from other kids when he's fighting the stomach flu, no matter how desperate you are to head to the semiannual sale at Gymboree.

8. **Don't go too far to be germ free.** Even if you keep your kid isolated in his Clorox-cleaned bedroom, your kid is still going to be exposed to something, sometime. I'm all for limiting kids' exposure to germs, but I'm also not going to go to extremes to do it. There is no reason to avoid the Hoppin' House or MOPS playgroup just because you're scared of germs. Go and have fun. Just take a squeeze of antibac soap as you leave, and do your best to make sure your kid knows that the giant foam blocks in the foam pit are for jumping on, not sucking on.

What to Do When the Inevitable Happens

My first major parenting fail happened when my son Joey landed in the ER for stitches when he was just fourteen months old. Technically, it was the coffee table's fault, so it shouldn't really count as a failure on my part, but since I wasn't paying astute attention when my little boy decided it would be a good time to take a flying leap into my arms, I'll go ahead and take 28 percent of the blame. Regardless, the second he hit the table leg, I knew it was bad. And when I spotted some white, shiny bone before the blood started to gush, I completely lost it. I panicked. I started bawling about how I hadn't been paying attention and how he was never going to heal and he'd have a horrible scar his entire life, and by the time I got done blubbering, my husband had already gotten a compress, stopped the bleeding, and loaded Joey into the car to head to the ER.

Accidents happen. I don't care if your safety repertoire involves custom-crafted foam protection pillows and a hefty supply of duct tape; your toddler's going to find the one weak spot in those pillows and hurt himself. And I'd venture to guess that the custom-crafted foam pillow supplier doesn't offer refunds. The lesson I learned from the fourteen stitches, five trips to the ER, one broken "eye socket," and a broken arm that I've dealt with is simple: when your kid gets hurt, stay calm and let your husband deal with it. Because as a general rule, guys are better at handling these things than we moms are. And when your kid is hurt, over-dramatic and guilty tend to cause more harm than good.

For example, if your kid decides to dive off the top of the highest point of the play structure at the park because "Spiderman did it in the book you read to me last night" and is now holding his arm limply by his side and complaining of a shoulder ache, your first instinct may be to run over to him, prop his arm up on the table while examining every inch, and scream for the lady across the playground to dump out her picnic cooler and bring you ice. But your first instinct is wrong. Because what you should do is pull your kid up on your lap and rub his back while busting out your cell phone and calling daddy so he can come take care of it. It may seem counterintuitive, but it's almost always your best option.

I've gotten so adept at this strategy that I hardly even flinch anymore when my kids get hurt. In fact, just last week, I heard a crash and went upstairs to find my four-year-old clenching her face, with blood spurting out between her fingers. Did I panic and start screaming? Nope. I remembered my mantra: call Daddy. I calmly grabbed a towel, pressed it to my daughter's face, and called my husband and told him I wasn't sure what had happened or how bad it was, but that he might want to hop in his car and come home because my calm, cool, and collected state was hanging on by a thread. And a very thin thread at that.

I sat there with a towel pressed to Kate's face, talking to her calmly while Cameron came home. And when he finally walked in the door and took control, I ran downstairs and spent several minutes panicking in my bedroom behind a closed door. And you know what? Throughout the whole process—through the ER wait and the stitches—Kate was calm. Kate didn't panic. And Kate didn't freak out about the fact that a pediatric plastic surgeon was using a needle to sew her face back together. And I like to take credit for her calmness.

Because, after all, I set an amazing, calm example by following my mantra: stay calm and call daddy.

Of course, there are always times when Daddy isn't available to swoop in and take over. And in those cases, you need to call Grandpa. And if he's not around, call your mom. And, if after exhausting all of your options, you haven't found anyone calmer than you to take over, you're going to have the hardest job of all: you're going to have to adopt a WWDD stance: What Would Daddy Do?

Adopting a WWDD Stance When Facing a Toddler Emergency

1. Stay calm.
2. Stay cool.
3. Stay collected.
4. Assess the situation while reminding yourself that you have to stay calm, cool, and collected.
5. If your kid needs medical attention, calmly explain to your toddler that you're going to need to get some help. Proceed to call your doctor (or 911 if necessary) and calmly explain the situation. Whatever you do, do not scream, yell, moan, or freak out. This will only scare your kid. (Note: Once you've gotten help and sorted this situation out, you can and should reward yourself for not screaming, yelling, moaning, or freaking out on the phone with your girlfriends. You deserve it.)
6. If you need to drive to the ER or doctor's office, see if you can find a neighbor or friend to go with you. It's best for you to sit in the backseat next to your child in his car seat for the ride so you can help him stay calm and comfortable. If this is impossible, strap your child into his car seat as calmly as possible, and give him a stuffed animal to keep him comforted.
7. When you arrive at the doctor's office, let the doctors and nurses take over. Your job then is to simply be there for your child and leave the medical stuff to the professionals. That and—you guessed it—stay calm.

I May Have Seen Something (Sort of) Like This Before

Before I sign off and move on to more exciting things (read: potty training), I want to give you some advice. Your pediatrician is a valuable partner with you in your child's health. And no matter how much you've read on Google about toddler health and safety, your pediatrician has probably read more. Which means you have someone super-smart on your speed dial to ask questions of when you need help. Your toddler's health is too important to trust to WebMD alone, so forge a strong, working partnership with your pediatrician in order to keep your toddler healthy. And to help you, here's exactly how *not* to do that:

Eight Things You Should Probably Never
Say to Your Kid's Pediatrician
1. "I really don't need your advice. I have the Internet."
2. "Well, you see, I put her on this beet-only diet to try to increase her vitamin C intake. What?! Beets don't have protein?"
3. "If I can make it to our appointment on time, then you can too. What were you doing, anyway?"
4. "I didn't bring him in earlier because my friend Sarah's mom's cousin is a self-proclaimed naturopath, and she told me that if I had her walk backward with her eyes closed, it would just go away."
5. "I know it's a virus, but won't antibiotics help just a little?"
6. "What's your take on the cookie diet for toddlers?"
7. "Thank you so much for providing all these tongue depressors and blood-pressure cuffs as toys for my kid. You know we get so bored waiting."
8. "She's more advanced than your other patients, isn't she?"

TEN

Potty Talk

*A Potty Training How-To
From Someone Who (Sort
of) Knows What to Do*

Hi. My name is Erin, and I am a PTF—a Potty Training Failure. Not only did I manage to un-potty train my son once he'd gotten it down pat (on purpose, mind you); I also managed to keep my daughter halfway trained for an entire year. Three hundred and sixty-five long days of sometimes potty, sometimes notty. Okay. That's not really funny. There's just something about this subject that makes me lose my mind.

All that said, you really shouldn't listen to a word I say about how to potty train your kid. In fact, you should probably read this entire chapter, taking careful notes on what *not* to do . . . unless you'd like to have someone to hold responsible when things don't go quite as planned. It's always nice to have someone else to blame when you're cleaning up pee from the living room floor for the sixteenth time.

Anyway, back to me. I have absolutely no excuse (okay, no good excuse) for being a potty-training failure. Get this: I used to work as a writer for a big parenting website, and part of my job there was to talk to experts—authors, psychologists, and doctors—about common parenting tasks, and then write articles to help our readers. Right as I started to potty train Joey, I was assigned a series of articles with Teri Crane—the Potty Pro. She has literally written the book—make that *books* (yes, that's plural)—on potty training. This woman knows what she's talking about. And I had her number on speed dial.

So, I decided to toilet train Joey as I worked on the articles—genius move, right?—and every day, as I hit road bumps on the potty-training front, I would call Teri and say something like, "Hey, Teri. So *hypothetically*, if there was a kid struggling to learn to poop on the potty, what would you do?" And she'd give me all sorts of wonderful advice that I would then apply not only to my articles but also to Joey's training.

My scheme (I mean my professional expertise and potty-training skill) totally worked. Joey was fully trained within a few weeks, with a snazzy new package of Lightening McQueen underdrawers to prove it. After that, I labeled myself an official potty-training diva, turned in my articles, and walked around for months telling anyone and everyone who would listen (my mom) how I'd managed to successfully potty train my toddler—a boy, no less—in just a couple of weeks.

My shoulder ached from patting myself on the back.

But then those cute little Lightening McQueen underdrawers started to unravel. Figuratively, at least. Joey liked his new potty-going skill a *lot*. Which meant I started hearing those six dreaded words—"Mommy, I have to go potty"—a *lot*. At bedtime, just as I finally beat the I-need-one-more-story-and-a-drink debacle, my dreams of a night on the couch with a bowl of popcorn would be destroyed by those six dreaded words. And at the mall, just as I managed to bribe Joey to sit in the stroller with a soft pretzel so I could look at shoes, everything would be ruined by those six loathsome words. And, the kicker, in the car, and those six dreaded words force me to brave—*shudder*—a gas station bathroom.

The final potty training straw came for me on a sunny morning in April. I had somehow managed to get both of my kids up, ready, out the door, and in the car at a reasonable hour. Both of my kids had clothes on (so what if Joey had applesauce on his T-shirt?), and both kids had eaten breakfast. I think I even combed my hair. I got the kids buckled in, threw two (mostly) packed diaper bags in the trunk, and headed down the road to go to MOPS.

I hadn't made it two miles down the road when I heard those six dreaded words. I squealed into the nearest gas station and ran into the mini-mart with a kid under each arm. I screamed, "Key! NOW!" at the clerk and raced into the bathroom. But my pride in making it that far without an accident was short-lived, because as my eyes adjusted to the dusty light, I saw the dingy, brown toilet and the filthy, wet paper towels on the floor. And I wanted to turn and run. But I also wanted to make it to MOPS without having pee all over my car, so I persevered. I piled fourteen layers of one-ply onto the seat and put on my I-mean-it mom face and told him not to touch a single thing. Nothing.

I grabbed him and held him haphazardly over the toilet, and there we stood for an eternity, with me balancing a pantsless two-year-old on one knee and a baby in my arms and a grimy bathroom key between my chin and my shoulder. And I oh-so-calmly cheered my newly potty trained son on as he squeezed out the teeniest, tiniest dribble of pee ever. I swear. Had he peed in my car, I doubt I would've noticed. And then he asked for a sticker.

My short-lived stint as a potty-training diva was officially over. Because I went back to the car that morning, scrubbed my kids down with antibacterial gel, and then dug a Pull-Up out of Joey's diaper bag. I put it on him, swearing that he was going to wear Pull-Ups in public until he was at least sixteen. I effectively un-potty trained him. And I'm not ashamed (okay, maybe a little ashamed) to tell you.

My potty-training skills only went downhill from there. When Kate started showing signs of potty readiness, I was in a busy time in my life. We were in the process of moving, and I was writing a book, and I figured that since (a) she was a girl, and (b) she had a big brother who was (finally) re-potty trained, she would probably just potty train herself. So, I bought her a pair of princess panties, showed her the potty, and let her go about her business. Five minutes later, she peed on the floor. The next day, we tried the same thing with the same results. Day after day, month after month, I sort-of tried to potty train her and—imagine this—failed to make any progress. Turns out most toddlers don't have the mental capacity or bladder control to potty train themselves. Who knew?

It also turns out that sort-of potty trained is worse than not potty trained or even un-potty trained. It's not a good place to be—especially when you have a kid who likes panties and wants to wear panties but can't figure out how to appropriately use panties, so she pees in said panties. It was a mess. But I've totally learned my lesson. When it comes time to potty train Will, I'm sure I'll nail it. Third time's a charm, right?

So, there you have it: I have officially established that I am not the person who should be teaching you to potty train your kid. You should probably talk to Teri Crane—or better yet, your mother-in-law. But if for some reason you'd rather stick with this PTF of a mom, here's my (somewhat adequate) potty training advice.

. . . .

Time-Out for Mom

For When You're Potty Training and Need Patience

"He says, 'Be still, and know that I am God;
I will be exalted among the nations,
I will be exalted in the earth.'" (Psalm 46:10)

Most High God, You are my refuge right now! I know that potty training is just a phase—but it's a long, messy and trying phase. I pray that You will fill my heart with joy and patience so I am able to instruct my child in a way that he listens and learns. I pray that You will give me the foresight to know what he needs so this can be a positive learning experience for both of us. Amen.

. . . .

Is My Toddler Ready?

I don't care if you bribe your toddler with a chocolate-covered puppy, if he's not ready to be potty trained, he's not going to pee or poop in that potty. I learned this when I decided all on my own (read: was pressured) to try to potty train Kate when she was nineteen months old. And I already told you how that turned out. Okay, so part of my failure was the fact that I put only a minimal effort into potty training her, but part of it was that she simply wasn't ready. She wasn't interested in the potty. She wasn't interested in potty books. She wasn't interested in bribery.

Now, before I help you figure out if your toddler is ready, there's something you probably need to know about the baby-boomer generation: they were potty-training overachievers. Either that, or their memories about how early they potty trained their kids are slightly hazy. Regardless, baby boomers are really into potty training . . . and potty training early. This often equates to what I call "potty pressure," the strange phenomenon where other people—especially *older* people—tell you that you need to potty train your kid without worrying about small details like whether M&M's have gone on sale lately.

I started feeling the potty pressure before Joey was even one. It started when a woman at church nonchalantly asked me if he was potty trained. And then she stood there with a big smile as if it were a totally natural expectation for a baby who couldn't even sit up on his own to manage to not only tell me he had to pee, but also to pull off his drawers and go in the potty all by himself. Yeah, right.

Anyway, right about when your kid hits the lovely "No! No! No!" phase, you may start facing potty pressure. This is very similar to the "Are you thinking of getting pregnant soon?" pressure that you've clearly already survived, so you probably have a fairly good idea on how to handle it. Your mom will mention—casually—that you were fully potty trained by the time you were twelve months old. Or your mother-in-law will say something like, "Wow! Back in the day, we just couldn't justify the expense of diapers for more than nine or ten months."

Let me save you a lot of frustration: Anyone who tells you that your kid can be potty trained before the age of one is crazy. That's right. I said it. Cray-zee. If your kid has the mental capacity and bladder control to be potty trained at one year old, then you should stop reading this book immediately and instead start filling out an application to get him into Stanford early admission. If not, well, then you should start looking for signs of potty training readiness when your kid is around two, give or take a few months. Notice I didn't say you should start potty training around two years old, I said you should start looking for readiness. At that point, you can assess whether you want to potty train based on a variety of other factors that I'll get to in a bit. Here are a few signs:

Ten Signs Your Kid Is Ready to Be Potty Trained
1. He likes M&M's.
2. He has a general understanding of the words, "If you do *that*, I'll give you *this*." If you're not quite at that point, go grab a bag of M&M's and see if you can get him to vacuum your living room.
3. He shows some interest in the bathroom and what goes on inside. (And no, an interest in pulling toilet paper off the roll and dragging it across the room doesn't count.)
4. You have to change his dirty diaper at close to the same time every day. Hey, they call it "regular" for a reason.
5. He can follow simple instructions like "Go get the toy" or "Come get an M&M."

6. He gives some indication that he has to go, whether it's going into a corner to poo or pointing at his diaper when he pees.
7. He knows words for pee and poop (or tee tee and poo poo or whatever you want to call it).
8. Target has a sale on undies with your kid's favorite TV character.
9. Your kid can pull his own pants up and down without (much) help.
10. The kicker: he is in a generally cooperative phase.

Are You Ready?

There's one more factor to a successful potty-training experience: You. Remember how I told you that kids don't potty train themselves? You have to help them. And just in case you're wondering, it takes a whole lot more time and energy to potty train than it does to change a few stinky diapers. The time-to-frustration ratio doesn't even compare. (And no, I'm not sure what a time-to-frustration ratio is.)

Anyway, another one of the (many) reasons I failed when potty training my daughter, Kate, was that I wasn't ready. I was in the middle of a huge writing project and a move and a bunch of other things, and my mind wasn't in it. It only amounted to added frustration. So before you start potty training, it's a good idea to assess whether you are ready.

Ten Signs You Are Ready to Start Potty Training
1. You don't see anything wrong with a little bribery now and then.
2. You have extra time to sit on the counter in the bathroom several times a day while your toddler tries to go.
3. You're not in the middle of a big work project or house redecoration or something else that is distracting and frustrating you.

4. You're feeling as though if you have to change one more stinky diaper, you are going to throw it on something. Or someone.
5. You're feeling ready to potty train—because you want to and not because anyone is pressuring you.
6. You have your husband's support.
7. You like M&M's.
8. You've prayed for wisdom, patience, and that your husband will take a few days off work to help.
9. You've become so immune to the smell of urine that you don't even mind that your house smells like pee.
10. The kicker: you are in a generally cooperative phase.

The Rules of Engagement

You're ready. Your kid is ready. It's time to get this potty started (*ba-dap ching*). I was going to write you a step-by-step list of how-to's, but then I realized that no two potty training experiences are the same. And what should be the first step for you could end up being step 948 for me. So, with that in mind, I decided to write you a list of potty-training rules. Rules that, if followed, could result in successful potty training; likewise, they are rules that, if broken, could also result in successful potty training.

Rule #1: Choose the Right Potty

Choosing a potty can be overwhelming, not only because there are approximately 1 billion (or maybe more like twelve) types of potties, but also because you will need a different type of potty depending on (a) your child's gender, and (b) your personal cartoon character tastes. If you have a boy, you're going to want a potty that has a big (make that huge) spray shield on the front. My first potty choice for Joey was just one of those squishy ones that you put on top of your real toilet. It was great—if you like that sort of thing—but I found out that it was lacking the essential element when I was on a conference call for work. And I had forgotten to press mute. Needless to say, I replaced that seat fairly quickly with a floor-model potty that boasted the biggest spray shield on the market.

Rule #2: Make Much Ado About Drawers

Little tiny white panties with pink bows. Tiny boxer briefs with robots. Seriously, there is nothing cuter than a toddler in drawers. Which is a good thing, because you need to gush and ooh and aah over those drawers enough to make your toddler feel as if wearing drawers is probably the best thing to happen to him since the day you brought home sugar-free popsicles. Because the more motivated your kid is to wear those drawers, the more motivated your kid will be to keep those drawers clean.

Rule #3: Pre-teach and Reteach

You know how the old adage goes: you can lead a kid to the pot, but you can't make him go. Or something like that. Anyway, if you just prop your toddler up on the pot and expect him to perform, chances are he'll get performance anxiety big-time. Instead, spend a few days teaching him about the potty. Check out some books on potty training from the library. Get a doll or stuffed animal, and go through the potty-training motions. Let your kid watch you or an older sibling go potty, and talk about what's going on.

Rule #4: Be Prepared

To fully embrace this rule, you have to understand potty training truth #254: no matter how active your toddler is, if you bribe him to go potty, he will sit on said potty until you make him move or until he pees. So, enter the bathroom prepared. Stock your bathroom with some books (for your kid), a magazine (for you), and several sippy cups of water (for when you get so desperate that you tell your toddler that if he swigs a bunch of water, something is bound to come out sometime).

Rule #5: Repeat This Mantra: Pull-Ups in Public. Pull-Ups in Public

I highly recommend adopting a "Pull-Ups in public" rule until you are 100 percent certain your kid can remember he's potty trained or until you've become comfortable explaining to restaurant owners that their handmade brocade seat covers have pee on them. Whichever comes first.

Rule #6: Keep Your Cool

I learned fairly quickly in the potty-training process that when I was stressed, angry, or frustrated about my kids' accidents, it caused them to be stressed, angry, and frustrated. And when my kids got stressed, angry, and frustrated, they often had more accidents—which, by the way, was the last thing I needed. I finally figured out that the only way to get out of this messy and pee-splattered cycle was for me to be the adult and respond calmly—even when I wanted nothing more than to throw myself into a massive toddler-style fit and leave the puddle on the floor for my husband to clean up when he got home.

Potty-Training FAQs

Question: My kid has been potty trained for over a year but still has to wear a Pull-Up at night or she wets her bed. What should I do?

Answer: Nothing. Yes, you read that right. Do absolutely nothing (except let her wear a Pull-Up at night). Some kids just don't have the bladder control to keep themselves dry at night. My son has worn underwear at night since he was two and a half and has never had an accident. My daughter still struggles to stay dry at night, and she's four and a half. I asked the pediatrician, and she said that many kids struggle to stay dry at night because they have small bladders and they sleep so deeply that they don't wake up until it's too late. She went on to tell me that while most kids are able to stay dry at night by the time they are six, very few two- and three-year-olds are physically capable of making it. Your kid will get there.

Question: When can I teach my son to stand while he pees?

Answer: Whenever you're ready to spend at least twenty minutes every day scrubbing pee off the cabinets, walls, and baseboards in your bathroom.

Question: My kid has no problem peeing on the pot, but he actually goes as far as asking for a diaper when it comes time to poop. What now?

Answer: Poop is harder than pee. Literally. (Okay, I know; I really need to stop with the potty jokes. Right now.) It feels strange for kids to have something literally drop out of their bodies, and that sensation often causes them to fear pooping on the potty. I think the big thing you can do is patiently talk to your kid about what poop is, what happens when it comes out, and why it's waste. Knowing is half the battle. If your kid is still struggling, one suggestion I've heard is to put your kid on the potty wearing a diaper so he can at least get the feel of what it's like to poop while sitting on the toilet. My friend Megan actually cut a hole in the back of her son's diaper and then set him on the pot. That way, he still had his diaper as a crutch, but he was able to see that when the poop fell in the toilet, nothing bad happened to him.

Question: I don't like the idea of bribing my kid. Are there any other methods I can use to motivate him to potty train?

Answer: No. Bribery is the only way to get your kid to do what you want him to do. Just kidding! I found that using a sticker chart and giving my kids a star sticker every time they had potty success worked just as well as blatant bribery with M&M's (and I put sticker charts in the category of "positive reinforcement"). You could also try praise, hugs, kisses, clapping, and cheering.

Parting Words from a PTF

And there you have it, friends. My attempt at giving you advice on how to do something that (a) I am very bad at doing myself, and (b) have no expertise in. But you read it anyway, didn't you? And I bet if you're being honest, you probably enjoyed it. At least the part where I set the bar really, really low so that when it takes you 346 days to potty train your toddler, you can brag to your mother-in-law that you beat me by 19 days. And two hours. Not that anyone is counting or anything. Anyway, I wish you luck. And when you do end up mastering the art of the potty, will you send me an e-mail and give me some tips? I still have to potty train Will, and I don't even know where to start.

ELEVEN

The Christian Daddy's Guide to Parenting a Toddler

What Dads Need to Know About Toddlers

I've been putting a lot of pressure on you moms, haven't I? I mean, in just eight short chapters, I've managed to give you an all-out sermon on toddler discipline, I schooled you on toddler tantrums, and I even worked in some tough to-dos for potty training. And you're probably starting to wonder why I'm putting all this pressure on you when I've said nary a word to your husband. He is, after all, your kid's dad.

To my defense, this is a book for Christian moms. So I have spent the majority of my time focusing on you. But I am an equal-opportunity lecturer, and I know you're probably ready to hear a bit about what your husband can do to stop those toddler tantrums and teach your kid to pee in the potty. And with that in mind, I've put together the "Christian Daddy's Guide to Toddlers" to help give your husband the down and (sometimes) dirty details about what it takes to be a good toddler parent.

Of course, I'm a mom. I know very little about how dads feel about toddler parenting. And as we learned in *The Christian Mama's Guide to Having a Baby*, the way dads think isn't always in line with the way we think. I mean, it probably should've gone without saying that it's a bad idea to rent a DVD player "so you won't be bored" while your wife is in labor, but for some sweet, albeit occasionally misguided, men (read: my husband), that was a core concept in their pregnancy education. So, once again, I asked my panel of "expert" dads to weigh in on the things they've learned since they became toddler parents. Some of it's not pretty—because we all know that the daddy learning curve is steep—but all of it is real. And hopefully really helpful to your husband as well. So, go ahead and hand over your book to your hubby for a while (that, or keep reading and take careful notes on how you can lecture him later) because we're ready to begin.

But first, let's meet our panelists:

Peter is the proud daddy of two—a toddler daughter and a newly adopted son—and a campus minister who is not only brave enough to take his kids to work with him but is already teaching his three-year-old the art of evangelism. And to play a mean solo on the guitar.

Troy is a returning panelist who, in just a few short years, has added two—yes, two—additional babies to his family, landing himself in the fun-yet-terrifying situation of being dad to three kids under five. And with this transition, he has not only become incredibly adept at holding a baby while playing freeze tag and tea party simultaneously, but he's also (finally) managed to master the Diaper Genie.

Cameron (yep, that's my husband) told me at least seven times that he thinks it would be "fun" to be a stay-at-home dad. He never forgets to make Saturday morning pancakes or give the kids their daily dose of horsey rides—however, remembering to take out the garbage? Well, that's another story.

Ron is a brave dad seeking simplicity who not only—get this, moms—is a stay-at-home dad to his precious daughter but does it while building his own personal writing career. All that and he says he's lived several lifetimes so far—the current one being since he brought home his beautiful gift of a daughter, Ella, from Russia in 2007. He's never had a cat, but since a cat has nine lives, he's wondering what could be next.

What They Think You—and Your Husband—Need to Know

Troy on Noise (or the Lack Thereof)

Toddler Lesson #249: Train your ears to pay astute attention to noise in your house.

I've learned the hard way that I should constantly be listening for any noise that doesn't sound normal. Before I had a toddler, I assumed a small scratch or clanging sound usually meant a creak in the house or a squirrel running across the roof. But not anymore. I now know that odd noises are almost always significant.

For example, just last week I heard a very faint clanking sound coming from the pantry. For a moment, I assumed it was the air-conditioning vent blowing on something in there, but since I'm a dad and I've become attuned to strange noises, I investigated. And found my twenty-month-old—who, by the way, was supposed to be resting in her room—standing on a stool behind the closed pantry door, eating peanut butter out of the jar with a *knife*.

This morning the noise was a faint scratching sound. Probably just a tree branch rustling in the wind, right? But I knew better, so

I dragged myself up off the couch to investigate and found my son using a pair of scissors to carve designs into the coffee table.

But the most important lesson I've learned is that the worst sound of all is the sound of silence. Dads out there, I implore you to never, ever be fooled by silence. No, your kid did not suddenly develop a fondness for sitting quietly and looking at picture books. Your kid did not magically fall asleep on his own or decide to play the quiet game. Without exception, if your toddler is not in the room with you and you're hearing silence, then you know there is trouble. I have found entire dressers unloaded and boxes of Q-tips spread all over the house, all because I ignored five minutes of silence. If they are silent, they are making a mess. It's that simple.

Peter on Being a Stay-at-Home Dad

Toddler Lesson #872: Maybe staying home
isn't as easy as I thought it was.

I have a confession—and please don't tell my wife I said this—staying home with the kids is much harder than going to work every day. In theory, staying home with the kids seems like such an easy thing to do—like Saturday morning, only without your wife there to pick up after you and manage the schedule. So when my wife got a job that required her to work on Monday mornings, I was quick to volunteer. I'd watch the kids while she worked. Her valiant knight in shining armor to the rescue!

I woke up early on my first day of stay-at-home dad-dom with high expectations. I was going to go on a morning jog with the stroller; then I'd make something fancy, like crepes, for breakfast and really show my wife's typical toast-with-peanut-butter cuisine up. Then I figured my daughter and I would do something academic—maybe math or chemistry—while my son slept, followed by a family jam session. It was going to be the perfect daddy day.

Or not. Let's just say my jog lasted six minutes, nap time five, and we had Cheerios—without milk—for breakfast. Seriously, when you're home alone with the kids, you turn your back for ten seconds to check the football score, and when you turn back, you'll find Rice Krispies—or something worse—in a trail across the carpet. And if you think staying home equates to time to kick back with your iPad while your kids play quietly on the floor, well, you're wrong. The words "toddler" and "play quietly" simply can't coexist in the same sentence.

Anyway, I love my kids. I realize that my busy work schedule doesn't even compare to what my wife does every day. I'm not saying I couldn't do it—because I know I could—but I also know that it's a lot harder than it looks. And for that, our wives deserve a lot of appreciation. That and a good back massage every now and then.

Troy on Putting the Kids Outside

Toddler Lesson #1361: Sometimes the dog needs to go out, and so do the kids.

I've done it, dads! I've discovered the secret to a calm house, a happy wife, and well-behaved kids. And while I should find a way to patent my secret and make a billion dollars from my brilliant idea, I've decided to just give it away for free. Because who needs a billion dollars anyway? That and this idea is just too good not to share.

So here it is: put your kids outside.

It's that simple. Next time your kids are running around the house as though you've given them a triple caramel Macchiato for breakfast—which, by the way, is never a good idea—just put them outside. Yes, open your back door, pick up your kid, and put him outside. If he's too young to be trusted not to eat beetles, you may have to go with him, but either way, put him outside.

Next time your kid throws himself on the floor in a screaming fit and starts kicking the wall because he wanted the blue sippy cup instead of the green sippy cup, put him outside.

And next time your kids decide to get into a massive squabble over the blue truck—the blue truck that is identical in every way besides color to the green truck sitting on the floor—put them outside.

And next time your wife has a complete and utter meltdown because she can't handle another minute of trying to make dinner, empty the dishwasher, and watch three cranky kids at the same time, put her outside. No, wait; I got that wrong. Put the *kids* outside.

Anyway, funny as it sounds, putting your kids outside is a great way to change attitudes—yours and theirs. Ten minutes playing in the yard and my kids seem calmer and are often able to handle themselves better. And I'm calmer too. The noise doesn't echo off the walls, and the fresh air seems to do wonders for a tense moment. And while it seems like a simplistic behavior management tool, it works.

Ron on Personal Expectations

*Toddler Lesson #1994: I'm a different dad than
I thought I would be . . . and that's okay.*

I didn't grow up with a dad around, so I had few stereotypes of what the role of a dad was. And the father-figure examples I did have were bad ones. Macho. Unfaithful. Confused. Abusive. As I entered fatherhood, I didn't know what manhood was all about. And I certainly didn't know what to do. What I did know (almost) for sure was that I was going to be the direct, no-nonsense, my-way-or-the-highway parent in my family. Leticia, my wife, would, of course, be the fountain of compassion and patience and mercy she had always been with me and the world. I would do my best to be our house's spiritual leader.

Now I know that I had a very unrealistic view of myself.

As it has played out, I have become the parent who is probably the most patient with my daughter, Ella. For some reason she doesn't seem to be able to press any buttons that make me react. Either I don't have any or there's just nothing she can do that really bothers me.

As Ella started to explore physical things—i.e., dive across playsets, leap from slides, and run ahead of my watchful eye—I've caught myself many times wanting to call out, "Slow down!" or "Be careful" or "That's too dangerous!" But something unexplainable inside wars against that safe, pragmatic voice and instead wants her to be better than my fears. I truly love her and want for her what I can't even imagine. Any limits I place would just slow her down.

So much for the direct, no-nonsense, my-way-or-the-highway Dad approach!

And that's okay, because while I envisioned myself as a disciplinarian, instead, I've become her cheerleader, her confidante, and her protector. For example, awhile back, she was playing in the backyard while I kept an eye on her (a very astute eye, might I add), and I heard her scream. She had fallen off the monkey bars. I raced out there to find blood dripping from her chin and her eyes wide in pain. Certain she'd bitten all the way through her lip, I went into "Ron emergency mode" and carefully carried her to the bathroom while repeating over and over, "You're okay! Daddy's here! You're okay!" I gently cleaned the wound, my heart racing as I envisioned a trip to visit the pediatric plastic surgeon for stitches. But as I tenderly cleaned the wound, I realized that it was only a superficial scratch.

I admit my gut reaction was to take my little girl into my arms and protect her—to keep her safe from the big, scary monkey bars and make sure she didn't fall again. But she wanted to play! And in my mushy daddy heart, I knew she had to get back up on those bars. So I talked to her. We talked about how she fell (she let go) and made a plan to keep her from falling again (don't let go unless your feet are aimed at the ground). And while I reacted in the exact opposite way of the tough, hard-lined Dad I thought I was, I'm proud to say that my reaction fit perfectly with the needs of the daughter God gave me. And I'm grateful for God's wisdom in giving my wife and me the personalities, insights, and talents to be the mom and the dad that Ella needs.

Cameron on Sibling Relationships

Toddler Lesson #2150: Sometimes all it takes to grow brotherly kindness is some attention from me.

My kids have had a love-fight relationship from the day Kate was born.

I still have the video of the day Joey walked into the hospital room in all of his twenty-month-old glory to meet his baby sister for the first time.

He pointed at his newborn sister and said, "Baby!"

"Yes, that's right, Joey! This is your baby sister, Kate!"

"Hat!" He smiled, pointing to the cute pink hat on her head.

"Yes, it's a hat!"

"MINE!" he shouted, snatching the hat off her head and running into the corner, where he played with the tiny pink hat—a toy that would never have caught his attention five minutes earlier.

And so their sibling rivalry began.

Now, I'd like to tell you that after a few bumps and squabbles, my kids became best friends forever and lived happily ever after, playing Star Wars tea party and Rainbow truck derby. But the truth is that after a few bumps and squabbles, my kids became best friends forever that lived to *fight* over Star Wars tea parties and Rainbow truck derbies. And I have to admit that I'm a little shocked. I mean, I know that my sole purpose in life as a kid was to torment my sisters (don't even ask about the BB gun incident), but I figured that with my spectacular parenting abilities (ha!) my kids would be the best of friends and not best frenemies.

After almost five years of dealing with all the brotherly love we have going on in our house, I've learned something that I think is pretty poignant: our kids' sibling rivalry is my fault. Well, mine and my wife's. Because our kids love us. They love getting attention from us. And they intuitively realize that while I am head-over-heels in love with each of them, I am also head-over-heels in love with their siblings. And that automatically marks their attention-stealing siblings with a target.

Anyway, whenever my kids start acting like Paris and company and squabbling over little things, I know immediately that it's time for me to take action. Usually that means giving each of my kids some individual attention. I'll take Joey outside to play catch or go to a ball game. Or I'll take Kate out for a daddy-daughter dinner or on a walk at the park. And usually giving them some individual attention does more than any lecture or punishment I could give, because they come home feeling important and special and ready to share some love with their brother or sister.

Troy on Coming Home from Work

Toddler Lesson #3371: Relaxing after work is a pipe dream.
Before I had kids, I had a vision for what it would be like when I arrived home from work every evening. As I walked in the door, my wife would float over to me with the largest smile on her face, thrilled to have the love of her life home; the kids would come running with joyful shouts of "Daddy!" as they hugged my legs. Then I would sit down with cold beverage on the couch and a kid on each knee as I relaxed and regaled my precious (and perfectly behaved) children with the events of my day.

Well, dads, my experience has been a little bit different. It turns out that the worst time of day for kids is, oddly enough, right before dinner. This also happens to be the time when I arrive home from a long day of work and the time when my wife is at her wits' end from her day. And let's just say that there is no floating, no kissing, no joyful shouting (unless you count frantic as joyful), oh, and no cold beverages on the couch.

These days, I walk into the door to find my wild-eyed wife giving me a look of utter desperation as she hands me a crying baby, tells me to ignore the toddler throwing a fit on the floor, and pleads with me to deal with my son who is up in his room because he decided to take the dog for a swim in the toilet (or some other equally inventive behavior). It is not what I envisioned—for sure—and at times, it feels downright overwhelming.

But I have come to realize a couple of things. First of all, my wife and kids need me when I return home from work. Like, they *really* need me. And as much as I need some quiet time to unwind after a long day, it can't always be my priority. I've learned to walk in the door with the expectation that I will be immediately thrust into toddler mayhem, and to do it joyfully—because I love my kids and love my wife and want to be the best father and husband that I can be. And sometimes that means dealing with a toilet-wet dog and a naughty four-year-old.

The Christian Daddy's Guide to Parenting a Toddler, in Summary (for Those Daddies Who Only Have Time to Read One Page)

- Noise—or the lack thereof—always, always means something bad is happening.
- When your kids fight, it's your wife's fault. Or something like that.
- If you need to unwind after work, do it in the car on your way home.
- When in doubt over how to handle a certain behavior, put your kids outside.
- The words "Staying home would be so easy!" should never, ever come out of your mouth. Ever.
- There is no such thing as "too creative" to a toddler. Especially when it comes to household pets, toilets, and whirring appliances.
- Never turn your back on your toddler—even for twelve seconds to check the score—unless you want to spend the rest of the day cleaning.
- It's okay if you melt to mush every time you see your kid. We know you were a crushingly strong, macho football player in your pre-kid days. And even if you weren't, moms love seeing their husbands as sweet, tender, and loving daddies.

TWELVE

Confessions of a Stay-at-Home Mom

How to Manage the Hardest Easy Job Ever

I consider myself a stay-at-home mom/working mom hybrid. I work part-time as a writer out of my home office, and I also stay home with my kids. And that means that while I often have 5:00 a.m. appointments with my MacBook Pro, I also have plenty of 5:00 p.m. meetings with the whine brigade. And—*shhhh!* Don't tell my working-mom friends this—I can tell you without hesitation that the days when I have a babysitter so I can head into my office to work are way (way) easier than my stay-at-home mom days.

Now, before all you working moms get all up in arms, know that I dedicated the entire next chapter to the crazy juggling life that a working mom leads. Because I know that it's not easy to balance life and work and kids and laundry, all while trying to be a productive worker and a good mom. And in fact, because I know you're busy and tired, I'm giving you this chapter off. So go pour yourself an iced tea and kick your feet up on the couch and relax for twenty minutes, because I think we all would agree that you need a break. Then come back in a bit and skip ahead to chapter 12, where you'll learn all about life as a Christian working mom.

Now back to you stay-at-home moms. The thing I've learned about being a stay-at-home mom is that it's the hardest easy job I've ever had. Staying home with my kids is easy because, well, they are pretty much the most amazing, sweet, and fun human beings I've ever met. I love waking up to sweet toddler smiles and sticky-armed hugs. I love that I can always take a break in the day to snuggle. I love reading books. I love telling my kids about Jesus. I love that I never (ever) miss a First—first steps, first words, or first fist-clenching, screaming tantrum.

But then there's the hard part. All those things I mentioned above—the smiles, the hugs, the books, the snuggles, the tantrums—well, they never end. As a stay-at-home mom, you get no coffee breaks. No time-outs for lunch with friends. No time to take a five-minute mental break and check out the sales on Zulily. I can't tell you what I would give some days for twenty minutes—*just twenty minutes*—when I could lock my bathroom door and take a long, hot shower without a single child breaking into my makeup drawer to put on lipstick or (worse) smearing said lipstick all over the new bathroom rug. That'd be heaven.

As a stay-at-home mom, there's just never any downtime. You working moms who are still reading this can attest: yes, you have long, frantic mornings and a jam-packed schedule, but once you get to work, all the crazy kid stuff stops. You never have to worry about anyone grabbing your coffee mug and screaming, "Mine!" or whether your coworkers are going to start throwing office supplies when they don't get their way. At least most of the time. But for a stay-at-home mom, it never ends.

The Christian Mama's Guide to Parenting a Toddler

Never ending as it is, I'm guessing that most of my stay-at-home mom friends would tell you that lack of coffee breaks notwithstanding, they love staying home with their kids. And while I already confessed that my workdays are my easier days, I'm also going to tell you they are often less fulfilling. Because even the best days at work are nothing compared to the pure joy that comes from holding my sweet babies in my arms—even at five o'clock.

I Love Being a Stay-at-Home Mom Most of the Time

I wouldn't trade my stay-at-home mom time for anything. Okay, I would trade some of the time—anyone want to trade me their Friday mornings for my Tuesday evenings at dinnertime?—but overall, I consider it a privilege that I have the opportunity to stay home with my kids. And—sorry to get all sappy on you—I know from experience that while the days are slow, the years fly by. And soon, my sweet babies will be big kids—big kids who will read their own books, make their own cereal, and refuse the mommy snuggles they ask for now.

Anyway, there's lots of reasons to love being a stay-at-home mom. And while the obvious reason is that you get to spend time with your kids—kids who grow up way too fast—there are other perks as well.

Ten Reasons Why I Love Being a Stay-at-Home Mom
1. It's perfectly acceptable to stay in my pajama pants until 10:00 a.m. No, noon. Okay, it's perfectly acceptable to label it a "pajama party" day and stay in my pajama pants all day.
2. Spending two hours gabbing with other moms on the playground is considered a productive day. Not only did you leave the house; you did something active.
3. No one will judge you for eating PB & J without crusts for lunch.

4. Finally an excuse to stay home reading all day. Okay, so reading *Gigi, God's Little Princess* isn't exactly the kind of reading I had envisioned, but it's reading nonetheless. Po-tay-to, po-tah-to.
5. A walk in the park really is a walk in the park.
6. I get to color rainbows and sunshine with markers and call it "playing with the kids."
7. I never again have to go grocery shopping on Saturday morning at ten. Unless, of course, I decide that grocery shopping with the kids isn't worth the effort.
8. I don't have to figure out how to use the timed bake feature on my oven, or worry that I somehow set it for a.m. instead of p.m.
9. Playing soccer with the kids counts both as a workout for me and an energy-zapper for the kids. That, and it's fun.
10. Two words: nap time.

· ·

Time-Out for Mom

For When You're Finding Joy in Being a Stay-at-Home Mom

"But blessed is the one who trusts in the Lord,
whose confidence is in him.
They will be like a tree planted by the water
that sends out its roots by the stream.
It does not fear when heat comes;
its leaves are always green.
It has no worries in a year of drought
and never fails to bear fruit." (Jeremiah 17:7–8)

Father God, I am so grateful that I have the opportunity to stay home with my kids. I love those small moments—snuggling on the couch while reading stories, rocking them to sleep, seeing their first

The Christian Mama's Guide to Parenting a Toddler

steps. And I pray that I will be able to find a sense of joy and purpose in the work that I am doing. My kids ultimately belong to You—and I trust that You are growing each member of my family into the people that You want them to be. Amen.

....

I Rarely Eat Bonbons

I'm sure you've noticed that there are a lot of people—especially in Christian circles—with strong opinions about working moms versus stay-at-home moms. I hear it from both sides. Many working moms I know feel that people look down on them for choosing to leave their kids in someone else's care so they can work. One of my friends told me that someone even went as far as to tell her that if she loved her kids, she'd stay home with them. Isn't that horrible? And if you're a working mom, well, first of all, you're not supposed to be reading this, but if you are, please know that there is no judgment here. There is no doubt in my mind that God calls some moms to be working moms and that He blesses those moms for following His lead.

Of course, the judgment goes both ways. Many stay-at-home moms take flack for sitting around eating bonbons all day. Because that's what you do, right? You sleep in (while your kids play quietly in their rooms, waiting for you to wake up) and have a gourmet breakfast (the kids enjoy it next to you, with impeccable manners). Then you enjoy your coffee and quiet time on the patio (while the kids read), followed by a leisurely lunch with friends at the country club and an afternoon of eating bon bons while soaking your foot in a personal foot spa. Wait! That's not how you spend your stay-at-home mom days?

Okay, I admit that while the occasional bonbon has crossed my lips (they are so good!), most of my stay-at-home mom days are jam-packed with business. I frantically try to keep the house (somewhat) clean and the kids (somewhat) fed while trying to attend to their educational and emotional needs. I rarely have time to eat lunch, much less sit on the couch, eating bonbons.

Which leads me to my next point of contention: many stay-at-home moms are judged as if they are wasting their time and their talents. This is not true. Every single stay-at-home mom I know is intelligent, talented, and driven. My stay-at-home mom friends have goals for their lives—they have dreams, they have ideas, they have hopes for their own futures. But they've chosen to put that on hold for a season, to stay home with their kids. It's a high calling, and I have so much respect for moms who do it.

I think we Christian mamas need to call a truce. There is no doubt that each and every one of us loves our kids fiercely. And there is no doubt that each and every one of us wants what's best for our kids. And for some families, what's best means mom stays home. For other families, mom works. And there are more options—everything from dad stays home to the crazy work-and-stay-home-hybrid situation that I try to pull off. Regardless, I think we all need to admit that we have no clue in what direction God has called our working mama compadres and stop the judgment.

I'm Only Really Frantic During Unhappy Hour

If you put a hidden video camera in my house (yes, that would be kind of creepy), you would notice that 98.4 percent of the meltdowns in our house—mine and the kids—happen after 5:00 p.m. This is the hour I like to call "unhappy hour." My typical days are pretty normal—a glass of spilled milk here, a sibling squabble there, but overall, we do pretty well. We play outside. We go on walks. We read books. We build block towers. We talk and laugh and tickle and smile.

But then unhappy hours hits. It usually sneaks up on me. I'll glance up at the clock and notice that it's 4:59 and think to myself unsuspectingly that I may want to start thinking about dinner. So, I'll tear myself from a riveting game of Duplo blocks and head to the kitchen to see if there is anything (a) easy, (b) healthy, and (c) tasty in the fridge. Naturally, there won't be, so I'll come up with an elaborate plan to use last night's leftovers in conjunction with the ground turkey that needs to be used to create a "super-fun dinner smorgasbord." This plan will, of course, be instantly rejected by anyone under six not only because it "sounds yucky" but also because "we did that last week, and it wasn't super fun at all."

With my unhappy hour mood already escalating, I'll toss the ground turkey in the pan to brown while trying to find those "toddler-proof" crayons I bought on clearance last week. Ten minutes later, I'll find them, only to realize two minutes later that my definition of "toddler-proof" and the box's definition of "toddler-proof" are clearly quite different. I'll pick wax chunks out of Will's teeth while trying to find something that resembles produce in the back of the fridge. And in a short-lived successful moment, I'll find a jar of applesauce. Score!

But my elation will be short-lived when I realize the turkey is burning. I'll toss bowls of applesauce at my hungry and whiny kids, and in a momentary gap in judgement, I'll decide that Will is probably old enough to start feeding himself. He is fifteen months old, after all. So, I'll give him his very own bowl—big-kid spoon and all—and get back to my turkey concoction.

And then my husband will walk in the door.

To a puddle of applesauce on the floor, Duplo blocks strewn across the living room, burned turkey-and-something on the stove, and me with glaring eyes, daring him to say something to me about the mess.

Which he does.

And at that point, it'd probably be best if you turned off the video. Because let's just say that unhappy hour rarely ends happily. I'd be a bit embarrassed if you saw how I sometimes act at 5:42 on a Tuesday night. Let's just say I'm not at my best.

It really is uncanny how a great day can dissolve into such a mess in the hour before daddy gets home. I've contemplated this often and decided to blame it on a combination of low blood sugar and mommy exhaustion. And even though our family's unhappy-hour meltdowns are certainly not *my* fault, I have found that a few tricks by me can lead to a much happier evening.

Five Tips for Making Unhappy Hour Somewhat Happy

1. **Plan dinner ahead**. Many of my unhappy-hour failures are the result of trying to figure out dinner while watching cranky kids at the same time. By simply making a plan for each night's dinners on Sunday, I've eliminated a lot of the what-am-I-going-to-make panic. I've also eliminated the words "turkey surprise" from my vocabulary, which my husband certainly appreciates.

2. **Start cooking during naps**. I used to guard my precious nap time with my life—no one (and I mean *no* one) was going to infringe on the only forty-five minutes of downtime I got every day. But then I realized that my Pinterest habit was derailing unhappy hour, so I made a vow to at least start prepping dinner during nap time. If you can, assemble lasagna or chop veggies when your kids are resting. That way, when unhappy hour rolls around, you'll be able to throw a few things in a pan still fully focus on the whiny child that's clinging to your legs, shouting, "My mommy! Mine!"

3. **Have a few surprises on hand**. This is my best trick, and it's a doozy if I do say so myself. I keep a plastic bin on the top shelf of my pantry, and it has a few "unhappy hour only" toys. I fill it with special markers and coloring books for my bigger kids and with special toys for Will. Desperate times call for desperate measures, so I only pull out the box during unhappy hour. And only when I feel a massive mommy meltdown coming on.

4. **Don't be afraid to quit**. There is no shame in turning off the

burner, moving that chicken parm aside, and making turkey sandwiches for dinner. In fact, I consider it a brilliant date-night-in-the-making. While your kids are eating "breakfast for dinner" (aka cereal with milk), you can run and change into something cute and then surprise your husband with a post-bedtime "date night," where you make chicken parm together. You planned it all along, didn't you?

5. **Give your kids a snack**. My mom never, ever let me snack before dinner, so I used to adhere to the "you're going to ruin your dinner" philosophy and make my kids fast during unhappy hour as I desperately tried to get something edible onto their plates. But hungry kids are cranky kids. And I've discovered that a pre-dinner snack—try making a plate with sliced apples, (cut) grapes, and pea pods—is often what they need to quell the crankiness until dinner is ready.

I *Really* Need a Break

My husband—I love the man, but he sometimes is a bit clueless about what life is like as a stay-at-home mom. And so, when he casually mentioned a few weeks ago that he didn't understand why I was falling behind on the laundry when I had "at least an hour every day when the kids were napping," I might have lost it a little. Okay, I totally lost it. Because the truth is that all these little tiny tasks—wiping noses, making breakfast, folding laundry, picking up toys—really are simple, easy things. But when they're piled one on top of the other for hours and hours, it gets exhausting. And by the time daddy gets home, I really need a break.

I sometimes start to feel a bit selfish to expect a kid-break after being home all day when my husband has to deal with deadlines and bosses and meetings. Because truthfully, he deserves a break too. But gone are the days when we ordered a pizza and propped our feet up at 5:30 p.m. without worrying about a single thing for the rest of the night. So we've had to get creative—and communicative—about what we each need after a busy day.

My friend Emily has worked out a system with her husband where he gets thirty minutes off right after the family finishes dinner. He goes into his office and closes the door and spends a half hour decompressing. In exchange, he takes over after that and does bath time and bedtime stories so Emily can get some much-needed downtime. You can also use weekends for stay-at-home mom breaks. My friend Rachel's husband, Jonathan, whisks the kids out the door on Saturday mornings to go for a doughnut breakfast so Rachel can sleep in. I confess: when I heard about that, I might have repeated the story to my husband in a totally obvious attempt to get him to do the same.

God's Calling

I still hold to my assertion that staying home is hard. And on many days, it's harder than going to work. (It's a good thing my working mama friends aren't reading this anymore, isn't it?) But the truth is that what's harder or what's better isn't important (remember: we're calling a truce). What's important is that each of us walks forward every day doing what God has called us to do—regardless of how exhausting it is or hard it feels. And what's more, God called us to do it joyfully—even on those days when you've done nothing but change dirty diapers and wipe up spilled apple juice.

To help you get through those long days intact, here a few of the verses that encourage me to be a joyful mom, even when I'm feeling anything but. Write them on a card you stick to your refrigerator—for easy access during unhappy hour—but most important, write them on your heart. It sounds cheesy, but truly, the only way we can live joyfully is to cast everything onto the One who brings us joy.

"Love the LORD your God with all your heart and with all your soul and with all your strength. These commandments that I give you today are to be on your hearts. Impress them on your children. Talk about them when you sit at home and when you walk along the road, when you lie down and when you get up." (Deuteronomy 6:5–7)

"But seek first his kingdom and his righteousness, and all these things will be given to you as well." (Matthew 6:33)

"He who began a good work in you will carry it on to completion until the day of Christ Jesus." (Philippians 1:6)

THIRTEEN

Confessions of a Working Mom

Ten Rules to Help You Find
Balance Between Work and Life

L ife as a working mom is a lot like cooking a seven-course meal for very demanding diners. You start out thinking things are going to be easy. You start dicing onions and browning meat and boiling water for pasta all while thinking about how much you love to cook. But then you remember that you need to make soup for the first course and you accidentally used all the onion in the sauce, and as you frantically try to find a substitute for onion, you realize you plumb forgot about dessert. Then as you head out to try to buy something from the bakery that looks at least semi-homemade, you realize the oven needs to be turned on in fifteen minutes and there's no way you'll make it back from the store in time, and before you know it, you're hiding the pan of burned sauce in the oven and serving PB & J and leftover cheesy mac to your guests.

It's hard to keep all your balls in the air. As working moms, we not only have to keep our "work" ball off the floor, but we also have to keep our "kid" ball safe and our "marriage" ball front and center. And then, every so often, someone throws a curveball at us and we're suddenly juggling "overtime" and "guilt" and "family issues" and "the PTA carnival that no one else can organize." And we're left feeling overwhelmed, underappreciated, and incapable.

I'm a working mom. A few months after my first was born, I took a job as a writer at Nickelodeon. It was my dream job. I not only got to work from home, but I got to write about my baby, a subject that was front and center in my mind 24/7 anyway. And as I excitedly signed the papers to start my new role, I remember thinking about how easy-peasy everything was going to be. I was going to work while my baby was napping, and when he was awake, I'd be able to dedicate my full attention and energy to being a mom. I'm sure you can guess how that worked out for me.

It must have been my second or third day of work that my "work-life balance" ball went crashing to the ground. Joey had woken up early from his nap right when I had scheduled an orientation call with my new boss. Joey was grumpy and hungry. I was frantic and frazzled. And let's just say that nobody—not Joey, not my new boss—saw my best side that afternoon. I'm lucky I kept the job for more than five minutes.

Anyway, I learned pretty quickly that seemingly brilliant ideas like "I'll just crank out these spreadsheets while the baby naps," or "I'll just put my line on mute and no one will hear my kid whining" are actually not brilliant at all. Because what seems feasible by super-mom standards is usually almost impossible by human standards. And I'm just going to save you the trouble of learning things the hard way like I did and tell you right now: all the rules change when you're a working mom. Everything you've previously known about work and motherhood collide into one giant, busy mess of meetings and daycare drop-offs and overflowing calendars.

The rules have changed, and that means you need a new rulebook

The Christian Mama's Guide to Parenting a Toddler

to get you through. And, since you know I love you (and happen to be in desperate need for some work-life balance help myself), I polled my working mom friends to get their best advice. Together, we compiled ten rules all working moms need to know. Just for you. (Well, for you and for me.)

. . . .

Time-Out for Mom

For When You're Juggling a Crazy-Busy Schedule

"Finally, brothers and sisters, whatever is true, whatever is noble, whatever is right, whatever is pure, whatever is lovely, whatever is admirable—if anything is excellent or praiseworthy—think about such things." (Philippians 4:8)

Lord God, I am so busy! I have a million things on my schedule and only a few hours to get them done. But God, I pray that throughout my crazy busy days, I am able to find quiet moments where I focus on the good, noble, right and pure things in life. I thank You for blessing me with a job and a family and so many good things and I praise You that You give me the capability to handle everything that You set out before me. Amen.

. . . .

Ten Rules Every Working Mama Should Follow

Rule #1: Don't be afraid to break the rules.

You know who you are: you're the girl who can do it all. You have an amazing family, a hunky man at your side, and the cutest kid that has ever uttered the words "Mama rocks!" Plus, you have an awesome job and you're looking pretty rockin' awesome in your mom jeans these days too. Girls like you, well, you're not afraid to break all the rules. And that means if you need to work for an extra half hour and then go to IHOP for dinner (again) so you can avoid emptying the dishwasher (again), then that's fine. No, it's better than fine. It's rockin' awesome.

Okay, so I may have morphed into an (overly) peppy cheerleader while writing that last paragraph. But I know who I'm talking to: I'm talking to moms who take their kids to church every Sunday. Moms who read books to their kids for twenty minutes every night and give them veggies every day. Moms who, in their wildest dreams, would never eat Marshmallow Fluff from the jar with their fingers. And I know that telling you—the mom who does everything right— to break the rules will inspire good-girl revolt if I don't season my words with a lot of grace.

And grace you will have! It's okay to break the rules sometimes. It's okay to go to work late if your kid was up all night with the stomach flu. It's okay to throw a bag of Cheerios and a cheese stick into your toddler's lunch box and call it a meal. It's okay to have three lattes and one doughnut all in one day in order to survive one of those six-meeting afternoons or a last-minute project. Hard as it is, these rules are meant to be broken. And that's why my number one rule for working moms is that you can give yourself permission to break the rules from time to time in order to keep your sanity.

Rule #2: Find child care that works for you.

When my friend Denise decided to go back to work, she immediately started calling local day cares to try to find an open spot for her son, Anthony. And she found one—at a day care that her friend loved that was right down the street from her house. It seemed like the perfect situation...to everyone but Denise. She just didn't feel right about it, and the day before she was supposed to go back to work, she pulled out of her spot at the day care. It took some finagling to find a different situation last-minute—and she actually had to start working a week later than she had planned—but in the end, she found a friend of a friend who ran an in-home day care. It's worked out great for her.

My point is that you need to come up with a plan that works for you and your family, and that may mean traditional day care. Or it may mean a part-time nanny paired with your mother-in-law taking the kids every other Tuesday and your husband going in late to work on Fridays. However you do it, you need to find a child care situation that you can trust 100 percent, because if you're even slightly worried about your kid, you're not going to be able to get any work done.

Rule #3: You can't do it alone, so don't even try.

I tend to be a tiny bit particular (read: controlling) when it comes to the way I like things done. And so, when my husband attempted to make Joey's lunch for school last year and not only forgot to put in fruit but he cut the sandwich into squares instead of triangles (which, by the way, is not the way Joey likes it), I decided it was easier to just do it myself. Daddy subsequently got banned from picking out the kids' clothes (doesn't he know that plaid and flowers do not match?) and fixing the kids' hair (no, a quick comb-through is not sufficient) and before I knew it, I was frantically in charge of every child-related task in our household.

Part of being a working mom is learning to let go of the things you need to let go of. Sure, your husband's lunch-packing skills will in no way match your triangle-sandwich-cutting expertise, but I bet that even with square sandwiches, your kid still has lunch. And you have five minutes to finish that report for the board meeting. Let other people—your parents, your coworkers, your husband— help you. It's the only way you'll survive as a working mom.

Rule #4: Build a partnership with your husband.

This rule goes hand in hand with rule #3, but I feel it warrants a special rule all to itself because your husband is your partner in life, which means he's your partner in *every* part of your life, including your working-mama life. Practically speaking, that means the two of you need to sit down and have a nice long talk about who's doing what and who's going where so you can keep track of your schedules and all of the to-dos that you both have. Emotionally speaking, this means you have a shoulder to cry on when you have one of those brought-the-diaper-bag-to-work-instead-of-the-laptop-bag days. Overall, this means you don't have to face long days, tight deadlines, your cranky boss, or your big promotion by yourself—because your man will have your back.

Rule #5: Get yourself organized.

In my pre-kid days, I blamed my messy closets and my occasional lateness on the fact that I had "my own organizational system that worked for me." And my special, self-taught organizational system *did* work for me (most of the time) when I only had two or three balls in the air. But when I became a working mom, suddenly my "I don't need to write it down because I have a good memory" plan and my "I'll just stack all the papers here and know that when I need something, it will be in the stack" strategy started to fail me. I needed help. And a good label maker.

As a working mom, you have to be more organized than you ever thought possible. Because if you don't, you won't be able to find the diaper bag right as you're about to leave for that all-important meeting that starts in five minutes, and then as you race out the door with your diapers in a ziplock baggie, you'll realize that the meeting is actually tomorrow and this is the day you were going in late to work because you had a dentist appointment that you have now missed. You need to get yourself a strong, consistent organizational system.

If you're anything like me, you may need help with that. I recommend seeing if one of your super-organized friends—or better, your super-organized mother-in-law—can come help you get your life organized. Sometimes it takes an outsider's perspective to help you see where you can slot every detail of your life. And if you do happen to be one of those people who keeps herself organized on her own without help, put down that color-coded life plan and come over to my house. I need all the help I can get. I'll let you borrow my label maker. (If I can find it.)

Rule #6: Get an assistant (or five).

My friend Dana told me that her best working-mom tip is to hire people to do all the work you don't have time to do. Dana has a personal chef make her meals and a laundry service pick up her laundry every week. I think this is a brilliant idea, and if you have the financial means to afford it, then by all means, you should hire a whole host of personal helpers. Like right now.

But, for those of us who don't have sixty-eight thousand dollars just sitting around waiting to be spent (which, by the way, is the average price of a personal in-home assistant, according to Mr. Google), hiring in-home help isn't always possible. As much as I'd love to hire a personal shopper to buy all my groceries (and a personal masseuse to ease the stress of being a working mom), I'm guessing my husband would get a little upset if I used our grocery money to hire a personal assistant. Or our mortgage payment to hire a live-in gardener.

My advice is to ease your burden to get help with whatever you can. Hire a housekeeper to clean your house every week or see if you can hire a service to deliver healthy meals. But don't go broke to do it. That means if you can't afford a personal laundry service, you just might have to convince your husband to help you fold the wash while he watches *Monday Night Football*. That or turn your kid's Onesie inside out so no one will notice that applesauce stain.

Rule #7: Do mornings at night.

It's 8:00 p.m. You've just spent the last hour (okay, hour and a half) bathing, reading, singing, and pleading your kid to sleep. Before that, you managed to not only cook dinner (with a whiny toddler clinging to your ankles, mind you) but also to avoid a massive sweet-potato-and-chicken-casserole collision at the dinner table. It was a successful night. And now that your kid is finally asleep, all you want to do is . . . go downstairs and pack lunches, do laundry, and get ready for tomorrow. Um, no. Shouldn't there be a rule that moms can't do anything after their kids go to sleep that doesn't involve a Kindle and a foot massage? Yes, there should be! But there isn't. And, as much as I hate to tell you that you should spend your precious evening downtime assembling PB&Js, you should probably spend your precious downtime assembling PB&Js. Because those workday mornings come fast—and often pass by in a whir of spilled Cheerios, missing socks, and last-minute phone calls.

My friend Kelly told me that she and her husband have a thirty-minute get-ready rush every night as soon as her kids go to sleep. She sets the timer for thirty minutes, and during that time, she packs her kids' bags for day care and makes sure they have clothes laid out for the next morning. She also figures out what they're going to eat for breakfast the next morning. At the same time, her husband makes lunches. Kelly says they usually get done with time to spare, but on the rare occasion their prep time takes more than thirty minutes, they cut it off, grab some much-needed R & R, and wake up a bit earlier the next day. Either way, they at least have a big jump start on the next day and still guarantee themselves some downtime as well.

Rule #8: Give yourself permission to slack off.

I call it the preschool walk-of-shame. It happens on those days when you've spent your entire morning changing diapers, scrubbing faces, and trying to convince your kid that scrambled eggs really are more delicious than cookies. And then, you get in the car and start driving toward preschool or day care, only to realize that not only did you forget to brush your hair or your teeth, but you also forgot to put on a bra. It's mortifying. And since I'm being all confessional, let's just say that I walked that walk my fair share of mornings last year.

I'd like to say this bugs me, but the truth is that I couldn't care less. I have the luxury of working in my pajamas (or in my pajama pants and a cute top on days that I have Skype meetings), so skipping the occasional morning shower isn't going to affect my job performance. Or my reputation with my coworkers. I take advantage. Getting myself showered and presentable in the morning is one area in which I can slack off, so I do. Likewise, figure out what has to go—whether it's your spotless kitchen or your kid's perfectly braided hair—and let it go.

Rule #9: Your kids always come first.

Confession: I really struggle with this rule. I love my kids desperately, but I also love my job, and I sometimes get so caught up in the task at hand that I push my kids to the side. In fact—and this is embarrassing to even confess—just yesterday, I let stress over a work project stand in the way of my care for my daughter. My four-year-old fell off of the slide in our backyard and broke her arm. I saw her fall and saw her arm twist in a funny way and knew immediately that she had a broken her wrist. Of course, I ran to her and held her and comforted her and put ice on the arm. But once she had calmed down, I actually considered—seriously—waiting until after a work call to take her to the hospital. Not my best parenting moment.

I did (after some internal deliberation) miss my call and take her to the doctor, and my wonderful boss was more than understanding about the missed meeting, but it frightened me that it had even been a consideration to do otherwise. Because as a mom, my kids always have to come first. Even when I have pressing deadlines or important tasks at work.

I want to make it clear—especially to you work-at-home moms— that I'm not saying you should drop everything every time your kid wants to play tea party. If that happened, you'd never get anything done. What I'm saying is that you should find adequate child care to make sure you can focus on your job when you're working and on your kids when you're not working, but when push comes to shove and your kids need you, they have to come first. Even when work seems more pressing.

Rule #10: Don't leave God out.

I *get* busy. I know what it's like to wake up at o'dark thirty and hardly have a moment to pee, much less take a break to spend time with God, until the kids go to bed. And I know as a working mom, those types of days are your easy days. On busy days, you work from sunup to sundown and then tack on a few hours of overtime after the *Late Show*. I know there isn't room on your calendar for one more appointment or one more to-do.

But I'm giving you another appointment anyway, because your relationship with God is (and must be) first and foremost even when—no, especially when—your life is crazy busy. And putting aside time to spend with God in quiet time can be the difference between a sane busy day and an insane busy day. But finding time to slot God in on your calendar just isn't enough. God wants to be more than a thirty-minute to-do in your life. He wants to be your everything.

My friend Rebecca told me she's been praying that God will bring himself front and center to her mind throughout each and every moment in her day. When she's doing laundry, God. When she's playing with her kids, God. When she's frantically trying to get out the door with her kids and her sanity intact, God. When I contemplated this, I decided that's a brave request. It's easy to toss God the bone of quiet time here and church attendance there, but to have God on your mind throughout the day, every day? That's a place where God can start to do powerful work in your life. And that's exactly where God wants to be.

God to Get You Through

So there you have it: ten simple rules, ten easy ways to make your working-mama life easier. But easier isn't *easy* by any means. In fact, easier is still exhausting and overwhelming, and before I move on to something a little more fun (yes, next up we're talking about mommy hobbies), I want to remind you that you have a God who understands what it's like to ache for His children, yet know that at times there are other things you are called to do than be with them. And as a reminder for you, here are a few of my favorite, uplifting psalms that have helped me get through busy days, long nights, and exhausting mornings.

"Be still, and know that I am God." (Psalm 46:10)

"Even in darkness light dawns for the upright, for those who are gracious and compassionate and righteous." (Psalm 112:4)

"Be strong and take heart, all you who hope in the LORD." (Psalm 31:24)

"My flesh and my heart may fail, but God is the strength of my heart and my portion forever." (Psalm 73:26)

"Cast your cares on the LORD, and he will sustain you; he will never let the righteous be shaken." (Psalm 55:22)

FOURTEEN

Get a Life

Finding Time for You in a World of Me, Me, Me!

Y ou need to get a life.

I'm serious. Get a hobby. Do something fun. Do something for yourself. Take a break every once in a while from the diapers, the talking Elmo dolls, the potty training, and the block towers and do something that's just for you.

Nuh-uh, you're probably thinking, *My job as a Christian mom is to cater to my children's every whim, making it so that my every waking moment is dedicated to their care, well-being, and spiritual health. And even if I wanted to take up pottery, it's not like I have the time, money, or ability to take on a hobby when I can hardly manage to fold my laundry.*

That's those pesky Mommy Guilts whispering in your ear again. And they are wrong. Because God doesn't condemn you for reading a novel during naptime instead of doing the dishes. And He certainly doesn't consider you less-than-adequate if you spread PB&J on bread and call it dinner because you were too tired to whip up a four-course feast. That just not how our God works. What a relief!

Let me remind you of this: Jesus didn't spend His entire waking life on earth working. There are countless examples in the Bible when He took time to rest, to relax, to converse with friends, and to simply enjoy life. And using Jesus as an example, I think we guilt-laden moms can do the same. I'm not saying drop everything and head to Tahiti to be a bongo drummer—your kids are obviously your number-one priority at this stage in your life. But having a number-one priority doesn't mean there's no room for you to have a life of your own. A life that goes beyond motherhood.

Nine Clues That You Need to Focus Your "Creativity" Elsewhere

1. You catch yourself shaving designs into your leg hair.
2. You've been trying to convince your husband that you should join a bowling league. Because if this morning's roll-the-ball session with your toddler is any indication, you have mad ball-rolling skills.
3. You rock out to "Jesus Loves the Little Children" in the shower—even if your toddler is nowhere in sight.
4. Your kid thinks pancakes with whipped cream smiley faces are a dinner food.
5. You take pictures of your block-tower creations—the ones you make while your toddler is napping—and text them to your mom so she can see what you did.
6. You start cutting your husband's sandwiches into cute shapes.
7. You've begun to consider makeup as a means of creative expression. And yes, neon orange eye shadow is totally appropriate for someone your age.
8. You're fairly certain that if laundry folding were an Olympic

event, you'd win gold. After all, no one can fold those tiny toddler tees like you can.

9. You add spinach puree to your brownies and actually think they taste "just like brownies."

If one or nine of those things sound familiar, it's time for you to get a hobby. Plus, now that you have a mature(-ish) toddler instead of a needy baby on your hands, you have the ability to do just that. I mean, chances are your toddler can probably play on his own for more than four or five minutes in one sitting. And if that's not enough, he's most likely weaned, or close to it, so you could even—*gasp*—leave him with a babysitter from time to time. Just imagine the possibilities!

Anyway, I want to dedicate this chapter to helping you reinvent the old you—to let a tiny part of your life reflect the pre-kid, chic, and hip woman you used to be—mom jeans and all.

Do It for Your Soul

It's so easy to push God to the back burner.

For me, it usually starts with a hiccup. A late night up reading a too-great-to-put-down novel or an early morning with a fussy child. And I'll set God aside, telling myself that I'll find time to pray tomorrow, when I'm less tired, less stressed, more focused. And tomorrow turns into the next day and the next. And before I know it, my relationship with God is on the back burner, languishing back there with the boiled asparagus instead of up front and center with the grilled chicken. Sitting in the back, getting stale and mushy.

And now that I've compared your relationship with God to a mushy vegetable, let me redeem that analogy by reminding you that God wants to be more than an afterthought in your life. He wants to move up there next to the grilled chicken—to be the main course and the substance in your life. When you're a mom, there are always distractions. There are dishes to be washed, toys to be picked up, towels to be folded, and boo-boos to be kissed. And those things are important. But so is God. And making your spiritual life a priority is the best way you can model Christ's love to your children. Here are a few ways you can make God front and center in your life.

Pray Humbly

You should see my prayer journal from 2007—back when I had two kids under two. Every single day, my prayers were the same. "Oh, God, help me to survive this day! Give me rest; give me peace; give me the fortitude to play *vroom vroom* one more time even though I don't understand the rules to the game." I cried out to God daily because I was exhausted and weary and needed Him to get through those long, drawn-out days.

I eventually even got to a place where my prayer journal included deeper thoughts, less-desperate pleadings, and spiritual revelations. But those prayers from my early days of motherhood still call to me from time to time—not because I'm still in that place, but because I clearly see my heart as I read them. I needed God. And I wasn't afraid to admit my desperate, pleading need for His help.

I don't think there is anything wrong with desperately crying out to God in our times of need. Or our times of joy. Or our times of passion. Even when we're doing the dishes and folding the laundry. And wherever you are in life, I want to encourage you to come before God humbly and ask Him for what you need. Because we serve a God who answers prayer.

Read the Bible and Beyond

A few months ago, my friend confessed to me that the Mommy Guilts were really attacking her. She loved reading, but she felt that reading anything other than the Bible wasn't a wise use of her time. So, she had banned herself from reading anything other than the Bible and an occasional very deep and theological devotional. I don't know about you, but that makes me want to kick those pesky Mommy Guilts to the curb once and for all! Because I love books, and anytime something is messing with my precious reading time, my claws come out.

Nothing can replace the Bible. It is my own personal glimpse into our heavenly Father and His living Word for our lives. I think it's absolutely essential for every Christian woman to spend time reading the Bible every day, learning and growing in our knowledge of God and His Word. But that doesn't mean reading other books is a waste of time. Far from it! I've grown significantly as a mom, as a wife, and as a Christian because of Christian literature—both fiction and nonfiction.

For me personally, I choose to keep one nonfiction book—a parenting book or Christian living book—and one novel open on my Kindle at all times. After my morning quiet time, when I spend time reading the Bible and praying, I make sure to also find time each day to read both of my open books. Sure, it may take away from my laundry-folding time or my Facebook-checking time, but reading books is something I love, and I'm not letting the Mommy Guilts dissuade me from this.

· ·

Time-Out for Mom

For When You Have a Bad Case of the Mommy Guilts

"Praise be to the God and Father of our Lord Jesus Christ, the Father of compassion and the God of all comfort, who comforts us in all our troubles, so that we can comfort those in any trouble with the comfort we ourselves receive from God. For just as we share abundantly in the sufferings of Christ, so also our comfort abounds through Christ." (2 Corinthians 1:3–5)

Lord Jesus, I am filled with guilt! And there is no reason, because You have promised us that You are a God of compassion and comfort. There is no room for guilt in You! I am doing the best I can as a mom, and while I want You to grow me and shape me, I also pray that you remove these feelings of inadequacy and make me whole so I can seek You completely. Remove this burden from my heart so I will be able to share abundantly in the comfort that abounds from Your love. Amen.

· ·

Hone Your Christian Relationships

I think I can pretty safely say that toddlers and meaningful conversations don't mix. My last attempt at going to coffee with a friend ended in disaster when my one-year-old managed to climb out of his stroller and onto a neighboring table. And since I was multitasking and trying to have a conversation while watching all three of my kids, I didn't even notice until Will had already taken a bite of a random guy's muffin.

It's a fact—proven by my own sweet children—that all children are equipped with a sensor that alerts them the instant you start to have a meaningful conversation. The sensor whispers in your kid's ear to start whining the second you pick up the phone to call a friend. And don't think you're off the hook if you attempt to do something insane, like go to lunch: that's when your kid will choose to do the one thing that you would never imagine he would do in a million billion years. Like climb on a table and steal a complete stranger's muffin.

But regardless of how difficult it can be to find time with your friends, I can't stress how important it is to have strong, Christian women in your life. Okay, I can stress it. It's really, really (really) important. I can tell you without any hesitation that my friendships with Christian friends have saved me again and again. These women have helped me grow. They've helped me learn. They've helped me cry. And they've helped me laugh. And while it's hard to find time with them—especially since they all have kids with little mom-is-doing-something-for-herself sensors as well—it's worth it. Every time.

1. **Go to kiddie places**. While the chances of your toddler not throwing a tantrum in a coffee shop are slim to none—even if you bribe him with a sugar-chip muffin—I can almost guarantee your toddler will have no problem in a baby swing at the park. Or in the toddler room at Jump-o-Rama. So, meet a friend and her kids at a kiddie place and show off your play-with-my-kid-while-chatting-with-a-friend multitasking skills.

2. **Go after bedtime**. A few weeks ago, my husband was gone on a work trip, so my friend Rebecca put her kids down to sleep, left her kids with her husband, and then came over to my house. We sat on the couch and chatted for hours in our pajamas, sipping decaf and catching up on all those things that we never have time to say or share.

3. **Exercise together**. Some of my best conversations have been while "running" with friends. (I put the word *running* in quotes because what I do behind the jogging stroller can hardly be called running; it's more like a combination of jaunting, walking, and heavily panting.) Plan to meet your girlfriends at the park once or twice a week for a "run," and use the time to catch up and get some exercise at the same time.

4. **Join MOPS**. I promise: I don't work for MOPS and am not being paid to recruit for them. But if I were trying to get you to join, I'd tell you that at MOPS meetings you'll meet dozens of like-minded moms who also have young kids and are dealing with all the stress that comes from juggling life and family and—here's the kicker—they'll watch your kids while you sip coffee and eat muffins and chat with said moms.

Do It for Your Spirit

I love art. Back in my glorious youth, I would visit art galleries and museums and spend hours staring at obscure works while chatting about things like color and tone and style and texture. And since I had time for things like sleeping and researching back then, I was able to actually sound somewhat knowledgeable when I talked.

Naturally, when my kids were born, my art gallery days became a thing of the past. Mostly because gallery owners tend to frown on grubby fingers touching their artwork, but also because my kids' taste in art is somewhat less sophisticated than mine. Joey considers the work he's done in his Star Wars coloring book on the level with a masterpiece. And so, when it comes to discussing color and tone and style and texture, they can't really keep up with the conversation.

A few weeks ago, my kids were at the table, coloring, while I did my usual pick-up-the-living-room-before-dad-gets-home-and-sees-what-I-let-them-do-to-the-house routine. And I had a moment of inspiration (or maybe it was desperation) when I grabbed a couple of crayons and a piece of paper and started to draw. It was silly, really—I think I drew a rainbow and sunshine and a couple of stick figures picking flowers—but that moment, that creative, artistic moment, reminded me of my love for art. And reminded me that picking up toys and fixing dinner simply can't be my only purpose in life.

Of course, the flip side to this is that I don't have the luxury of dropping everything and heading to an art gallery. So we moms have to find ways to be creative—to meld our hobbies with our busy family lives in a way that allows us to hone our passions while also being present as moms. It's tough. And I can't say I have all the answers. But, my friends on Facebook do. Here are their creative ways to combine hobby time with motherhood

Eleven Mom Hobbies . . . and the Creative Ways
Moms Make Them Work with Kids

1. **Cooking**. I used to love cooking—until cooking became less about the cooking and more about managing to get something

somewhat nutritious on the table with two kids clinging to my legs and a baby on my hip. But my friend Angie told me about her weekly Sunday afternoon cooking extravaganza. She researches recipes throughout the week and then heads to the store sans toddler on Sunday afternoon at naptime. She then spends the afternoon and evening cooking a fancy schmancy meal for her family while daddy's on kid duty.

2. **Quilting, Knitting, and Crochet**. My friend Ann told me that if you quilt in twelve-inch squares, you can work slowly on small sections. This means you can work on a small piece at night after your kids go to bed without worrying about leaving quilting supplies spread out across the living room, tempting small hands during the day. You could do the same thing with knitting or crochet, as both offer a great opportunity to work in small squares or blocks over time.

3. **Painting or Drawing**. My friend Amanda has set up an art studio in her house. Her toddler works on a masterpiece of crayon scribbles while Amanda works on her beloved watercolors.

4. **Gardening**. Here's something you may not know about toddlers: they love playing in the dirt. Oh, wait; you already knew that? Well, put that love to good use and start a garden with your kid. Choose a small plot and give your toddler a shovel or rake and let him "cultivate" the ground while you plant, water, and grow vegetables or flowers.

5. **Dancing**. Put on a pair of leg warmers, because your living room dance party just got serious. And I can pretty much guarantee you that you and your Jazzercise skills will become the highlight of your toddler's day if you play it right. Just make sure the music is loud and the furniture is pushed out of the way.

6. **Sports**. There is no reason to give up your kickball league or your soccer team just because you're a mom. My friend Jenna has her husband and daughter tag along to her weekly

volleyball games. Her daughter not only gets a huge kick out of seeing her mom play, but also gets to spend some fun one-on-one time at the park with her daddy while mommy gets her sport on.

7. **Photography**. Have you seen the book *When My Baby Dreams*? Adele Enersen poses her sleeping baby in a new way every day and then documents it with pictures. When I first saw the book, I thought she was crazy. (Sorry, Adele!) I mean, who has time to pose scenes with a sleeping baby when there is e-mail to check? But after spending some time looking at the pictures, I realize that she's creatively managed to combine two of her favorite things—photography and her daughter—into an art form and a hobby all wrapped into one supercute package. You can do the same thing! Grab your camera and your kid, and practice with different lighting, poses, scenery, and more.

8. **Writing**. You don't have to be a professional writer to write. In fact, I heard that the lady who wrote the Twilight series did all of her writing while her kids napped or played in the playroom. Anyway, my friend Alisha does a time swap with her husband. Every Tuesday morning, she wakes up early and heads to the coffee shop to write for two hours. Then, on Thursday, he's the one who gets up early and goes to play basketball with his friends at the gym.

9. **Scrapbooking**. I confess that the mere sight of a punch press makes me want to start hyperventilating. It's not that I don't like scrapbooking—okay, who am I kidding? I don't like scrapbooking. But some people do. My friend Nicole makes these absolutely amazing scrapbooks for her kids, and I know they will treasure the memories always. Nicole says that the best way to scrapbook when you're a busy mom is to collect little tidbits—ticket stubs, photos, stickers, pieces of artwork over time, and then pull it all out in one big chunk on an evening after your kids go to bed or on a weekend when

you have access to child care, because there's nothing more frustrating than getting right to the punch-pressing fun part and having to stop. Or so I've heard.

10. **Crafting**. My friend Abby wrote this amazing crafting book (*Crafty Mama*) and she teaches you how to make really cool projects out of things like toothbrushes, baby spoons, and wipe containers. I'm not saying I'd go as far as making a project, but if I were to suddenly get an urge to craft, I'd probably do something like invite several moms over to my house for a crafting party and rotate babysitting duties so everyone could get their crafting done.

11. **Music**. My friend Amy started taking violin lessons a few months ago—as a thirtysomething adult. She had always wanted to do it, so she just bit the bullet and signed herself up. Trade babysitting with a friend to take lessons, and then lock yourself somewhere quiet—the patio or attic maybe?—to practice your instrument.

Do It for You

You're going to thank me for this in a few weeks when you decorate your living room with your very own handmade, hot-glue-gunned lampshade. Or you score the winning run (or at least make it to first base) for your kickball team. Because by allowing yourself a way to express yourself—creatively, spiritually, athletically, and musically—you'll find you're more able to function as a mom, a worker, a wife, and a friend. I wouldn't lie about something like that—trust me; I never lie about serious things like hot glue guns. And speaking of getting a life, there's more: it's about time you started dating again too. Next up on our agenda is talking about how you and your husband can reinvent date night—and your toddler-parent relationship to boot.

FIFTEEN

Reinventing Date Night

Date Night Makes a Bold Return

ate night used to be the highlight of my week. My husband would grab me, arch me backwards, and kiss me passionately (okay, that never happened) and smile with a crooked smile as he told me to put on something cute because he was taking his girl out on the town. Then I'd slip into a cute little dress and super-high heels and we'd head off to explore some quaint little bistro or to listen to an up-and-coming jazz trio play. Okay, it maybe didn't go quite like that, but we'd at least have a quiet dinner together.

But date night with kids? *Simple, spontaneous, passionate,* and *fun* are certainly not words I'd use to describe it. It usually begins on Sunday, when one of us says something like, "Wow! We haven't done anything together in, like, two months. Maybe we should get a babysitter on Friday night and go out on a date." Then we start winking at each other and thinking about all of those simple, spontaneous, passionate, and fun date nights of the past that still had us convinced that date night was (a) worth the effort, and (b) something we could pull off and still have the energy to actually talk on said date.

And then the fun would begin:

Sunday night: I start by optimistically calling fourteen babysitters to see if anyone wants to earn a few bucks on Friday night. After getting no responses to my voice mails by Tuesday, I remember that most of my babysitters are teenagers. And that means they don't mess with old-fashioned things like voice mail.

Tuesday afternoon: I send a group text to all fourteen babysitters and get an immediate response from eight of them and then have to figure out who texted back first and who is just confused (which, by the way, is usually me).

Friday afternoon: I put the kids down for an early nap so they'll be well rested for their big night with the babysitter (and less prone to throw mac & cheese on the wall.) I tell them 2,342 times to try to fall asleep, and finally, after two hours, I realize it's a futile effort. The babysitter will have to deal with cranky children. And a cranky mommy.

Friday at 4:00 p.m.: I hand my toddler a brush and a stuffed animal and let him play on the bathroom floor while I get ready for date night. I frantically dry my hair, desperate to get it at least halfway dry before he gets tired of playing. I swipe on a coat of mascara and head to my closet to try on fourteen dresses, none of which fit now that I'm on the nine months on, fifteen months off baby weight loss plan. My toddler laughs. Mommy is funny when she's hopping around, throwing dress after too-small dress on the floor.

4:30 p.m.: I decide on jeans.

5:00 p.m.: Being the compassionate person I am, I decide to feed the kids before the babysitter comes so she won't have to fight that battle. I boil some pasta, add a few frozen peas, like a good mom; pour on the cheese sauce, and then hand it to my

The Christian Mama's Guide to Parenting a Toddler

kids, who promptly determine that they don't like mac & cheese anymore.

5:24 p.m.: I tell them that I don't care if they hate mac & cheese; they're going to eat it and going to eat every last bite, and they're going to pretend they like it. The kids laugh. Mommy is funny when she's frantically trying to wash dishes, slice apples, and force-feed kids all at the same time.

5:26 p.m.: Daddy walks in the door and grabs me, arches me backwards, and kisses me passionately. (Okay, really, that has *never* happened.) As I'm saying hello, a big wad of mac & cheese flies across the room and lands on my jeans. Off go the jeans—and not in the sexy, romantic sort of way but in the fuming-mad-because-now-I-have-to-find-something-else-that-fits sort of way.

5:28 p.m.: Daddy loosens his tie and gives the kids his infamous you'd-better-start-behaving-this-instant-or-I'm-going-to-do-something-really-really-bad lecture just as the doorbell rings. Hello, babysitter!

5:29 p.m.: We try to tell the babysitter that the kids aren't to have any sugar after dinner and that they can only watch a half hour of Dora before bedtime, but she can't hear us over the ding of spoons banging against the counter. We give up and decide that one night of sugar-and-TV-fueled mayhem isn't going to kill them. It might kill the babysitter, but our kids will undoubtedly survive.

5:39 p.m.: We pull out of the driveway, high-fiving each other that we have successfully escaped. I mean, left. We would never want to escape our kids.

5:42 p.m.: I ask him about his day. He asks me about mine. We both yawn loudly. Just as we start to merge on the interstate, we realize that the cute bistros and romantic jazz clubs feel very, very far away. And we're both very, very tired. We divert the car into the little Tex-Mex place in our neighborhood and order tacos.

5:56 p.m.: Famished, we finish our tacos in record time. We get refills on our sweet tea, but about halfway through, we both start to fade. It's not that we're not having fun—we are—but the sheer amount of energy it took to plan date night had stolen whatever amount of energy we had to actually go on date night.

6:21 p.m.: For lack of something better to do, we decide that if we have a babysitter, we may as well take advantage of the time. We head to the grocery store and pick up diapers, milk, eggs, and a carton of sprinkle-covered cupcakes from the bakery that we proceed to devour in the car without worrying about the sprinkles getting all over our faces.

7:18 p.m.: As we pull into the driveway, I wonder aloud if perhaps the babysitter had decided to put the kids down a bit early. Maybe she had managed to wrangle all three kids through baths, into their pajamas, through story time, and into bed by herself. Miracles can happen, right?

7:21 p.m.: Wrong. The kids are all sitting at the counter, eating ice cream sandwiches. Every toy in the house has somehow managed to make its way out of its appropriate place and onto the living room floor. There is mac & cheese strewn across the refrigerator door. The dog is hiding under the bed. And the kids are all wearing the kind of grin that tells me that I don't even want to ask what has happened while we were away.

7:28 p.m.: I don't ask. I fork more cash than we spent on dinner over to the babysitter, and she leaves. I herd the kids into the bathtub while my husband loads toy after misplaced toy into laundry baskets to be put away later.

7:48 p.m.: We finally manage to get all three kids into pajamas and through an efficient story time and into bed with warnings that there are no more drinks, no more trips to the potty, no more bedtime kisses, no more anything. Okay, just one more trip to the potty. But after that, nothing else. Except for a tiny sip of water. But after that, well . . .

8:22 p.m.: We both crash onto the couch and, with a sigh, turn on the TV. Date night culminates with an hour of *Top Chef* reruns, during which I fall asleep. Married with children at its best.

Time-Out for Mom

For When You're Praying for Your Relationship with Your Husband

"I am my beloved's and my beloved is mine;
he browses among the lilies." (Song of Solomon 6:3)

Father God, I belong to my husband, and he belongs to me, and yet many days we ignore each other, putting our relationship on the back burner in order to attend to less important things. Please, Lord, help me to make my husband a priority so that both of us can walk assured in the fact that You created our relationship for a purpose. Renew our love for each other, Lord, and unite us against the enemy. Amen.

Reinventing the Date

Now I've really done it, haven't I? In just a few short pages, I've effectively destroyed any and all optimism you ever had surrounding the return of romance to your marriage. I'm sorry! I didn't mean to do it. I'm just trying to give you a realistic picture of what you're facing when it comes to reinventing date night. And now that your hopes are shattered and lying there on the living room floor next to Bob the Builder and friends, I'm going to help you pick them up. Because having a romantic and passionate marriage is possible. Even with a toddler or two underfoot. Date night can be what it was before—no, wait; strike that—date night can be *better* than it was before. It's just not going to look the same as it did before kids. You'll have to be a bit strategic about it.

Are you ready to take back your marriage? To toss aside those PJ pants and slip on a pair of mom jeans (or if you're feeling super-frisky, some lingerie)? To trade Dino Nuggets and bedtime stories for romantic evenings à deux? I'm going to help you. Because through-out the next few pages, I'm reinventing Christian mama romance. Reinventing the babysitter, reinventing the date budget, and rein-venting date night. Perhaps I should apply for a patent.

Reinventing the Date Budget

Have you ever watched *The Bachlorette*? I (of course) would never waste my time with totally worthless reality TV, but if I *had* seen it, I would know that when the Bachelorette goes on dates, she does things like whisk her suitors away on hours-long helicopter tours of the city at sunset or on zip-line rides through the jungle. And I have to say that I'm fairly certain that if I whisked my husband away on a private jet to Tahiti, *Bachelorette*-style, it would definitely put him in a romantic mood. Until he realized that I had to sell our house to pay for it.

Shockingly, *Bachelorette*-style dating is a little out of our price range. Technically, once I've accounted for the exorbitant amount of money I spend on diapers, wipes, and Lego sets, normal dinner-and-a-movie-style dating can push our budget. And that's why the first thing I'm going to reinvent when I'm reinventing date night is the date budget. Because for most young couples, spending sixty dollars on a babysitter and an additional eighty on a fancy schmancy prix fixe dinner on a regular basis is simply out of the question. Here are my best tips on how to do date night on the cheap.

Ten Romantic Dates that Cost Fewer Than Thirty(ish) Dollars
1. **DIY tapas tour**. Even if you don't have a tapas bar in town, you can still do tapas the way the Spanish do it. Just head to your favorite restaurant and order an appetizer to share. When you're done, move on to the next restaurant and repeat. After three or four restaurants, you'll not only be full, but will have had plenty of time to talk and make googly eyes across the table.

2. **A dessert picnic**. Make (or buy) a gourmet dessert and head out to a park or scenic overlook to watch the sunset and enjoy the decadence.

3. **Go to a (high school) musical**. Sure, Broadway is probably going to cost you a bit more than thirty bucks, but why not go to a production put on by a local high school? And hey, if you happen to discover the Lea Michele of 2024, then you'll be able tell your kids that you spotted her first.

4. **Go to the museum**. Nothing says romance like a night at the museum.

5. **Play cards**. Whoever said you can't play pinochle post–*Mad Men* has obviously never sat in a coffee shop, sipping a latte, playing two-hand pinochle on a date night. And now I'm also reinventing cool.

6. **Go to the bookstore**. My husband and I got into the bookstore habit when we realized that our local Barnes & Noble not only had a huge cookbook section but it also had a lovely Starbucks on premise. It's one of our standby dates—and when we're feeling really rich, we allow each other to pick out a juicy new novel as a "date night treat."

7. **Split planning**. Hand your hubby a ten-dollar bill and see what he can plan with it and a bit of ingenuity. When you're done doing his activity, grab ten dollars of your own and plan the second half of your date.

8. **Take advantage of happy hour**. There is a Tex-Mex restaurant in Austin that offers a free "nacho car" on weeknights before six. You can go and load up on chips, ground beef, beans, queso, salsa, and more. All you have to do is buy your own iced tea. Kind of makes you want to move to Austin, doesn't it? Or at least check out which local restaurants offer special happy-hour food deals.

9. **Go thematic**. Pretend you're living in the '80s and go roller skating (leg warmers optional but strongly encouraged). Or head to a 1950s diner and share a milk shake (one shake, two

straws). You could even go "Italian" and share a heaping bowl of pasta or "New York" and get slices of cheesecake and then stroll your city's "central" park, hand in hand.

10. **Go dancing**. Even if you're a bit too old (or old-at-heart) for the club scene, it doesn't mean you can't go dancing. Google live music and see where an up-and-coming local band is playing, or simply park your car, blast the radio, and dance under the stars.

Reinventing the Babysitter

I'm going to need to spend a few minutes standing on a soapbox. Because I'm seriously shocked at how much babysitters are charging these days. I once had a babysitter—a high school student—tell me she charged twenty dollars per hour. Twenty. Dollars. Every. *Hour?* I'm pretty sure I didn't make that much money at my first job after college! Anyway, I want my kids to get the best care possible, and I want to pay my babysitters a fair rate, but I also feel there's a point that it's just too much. I used to charge something like a buck per kid per hour for babysitting. And I thought I was making a fortune! But kids these days, well, they ask for the moon, and we desperate parents who would do anything to get out of the house once in a while have no choice but to pay it. After all, the alternative is staying home.

Anyway, now that I've gotten that off my chest, let me just tell you loud and clear: hiring a babysitter is expensive. Like more than the cost of a new pair of (Old Navy) jeans. I asked a few of my friends what they typically pay for babysitting, and on average, people in my area pay around ten dollars an hour. My friend in California told me she usually pays fifteen. New Yorkers tend to pay upwards of eighteen an hour. Whatever you're paying, at average rates, it can easily cost you fifty dollars to go on a date before you've even left the house. Ouch.

I think we can all agree it's time to reinvent the babysitter. To help, I've spent some time polling my friends on how they find, hire, and pay for babysitters. I've quizzed them on their creative solutions. I've jotted down their best ideas. And I've compiled everything into this handy list for you to use and reuse. Here's how you, too, can reinvent the babysitter:

Eight Creative Ways to Find, Hire, and Pay for a Babysitter

1. **Start a babysitting club on Facebook**. My friend Karen started an Austin Area Babysitters Club Facebook group and invited her mommy friends to join. Then she asked all of the members to recommend their best babysitters. From there, invited babysitters posted letters of reference and an extensive questionnaire for the group. Now, when a family needs a babysitter, they post when they need help and the rate they are willing to pay, and recommended babysitters are allowed to "bid" on jobs by responding to the post. Easy, effective, and a great way to find a babysitter at a price you're willing to pay.

2. **Ask Grandma**. I have yet to meet a grandmother who doesn't love to spend some time with her grandkids. I used to feel nervous asking my mom to babysit—as if I were taking advantage of her—but she has reassured me again and again that it truly is her pleasure. And I believe her.

3. **Ask someone else's grandma**. Don't limit yourself to teenagers! Grandmas are notoriously great babysitters because they love kids—and miss their own grandchildren. There's a grandma in our church who just loves to babysit and is willing to do it at a much cheaper rate than many teenagers because she's in it for the kids and not for the money.

4. **Try a date night swap**. My friends Jan and Mandy do a date night swap. On Monday nights, Mandy heads to Jan's house after her kids are tucked into bed while Jan and her husband go out on a late-night date. On Wednesdays, they swap, and Jan goes to Mandy's house.

5. **Trade babysitting coupons with your friends**. Make and print several vouchers good for one hour of babysitting. Hand them out to your friends. Whenever you need a babysitter, trade coupons for hours of babysitting. When you run out of coupons, you only need to watch your friend's kids to earn coupons back.

6. **Go on a double date**. Go out with friends, and split the cost of the babysitter.

7. **Trade professional services**. I once traded writing coaching—a local senior needed help with her college essays— for babysitting. My friend is a hairstylist, and she traded free prom hairstyles to neighborhood teenagers for two hours of child care. Think about what you have that a teenager might want—blogging expertise, personal training advice, college advice—and then swap that for babysitting hours.

8. **Try a drop-off**. I admit it—the idea of dropping my kids off at a random place to play with random kids while I go enjoy dinner makes me feel that I wouldn't enjoy dinner. I'd worry about my kids instead. But, that said, I've recently discovered that fun kid places like MyGym and Little Gym and Gymboree offer Parents' Night Out events where you can drop your kids off for a fun night and then go off for your own fun night. Of course, check the prices before you plan an extravagant evening—in some places these drop-offs can cost as much as forty dollars per kid.

Reinventing Date "Night"

Even with your reenergized romance and the reinvention of your dating budget, you're still probably too tired to stay out much later than, say, seven thirty-two. And even if you wanted to stay out past seven thirty-two, it can be downright impossible for a babysitter to put your kids down on her own, meaning late-night dates can become a thing of the past. But I'm here to rescue you again. Because who said date night had to be at night? What about date "early afternoon"? Or date "ten o'clock on a Tuesday morning"? Or date "whenever Grandma is available to babysit"? Here are ten ideas.

Ten Romantic Daytime Dates

1. **Do breakfast**. I personally don't think it gets much better than eating a plate of hot pancakes with maple syrup. Except for maybe eating a plate of hot pancakes with maple syrup across the table from your hubby, whose hair is still tousled from sleep.

2. **Get sporty**. Even if you're not a sporty type of girl (and I'm not), it's fun and energizing to get sporty with your man. Head to the park to play a little one-on-one, or go on a short hike by the lake. On your way home, stop by the minimart to get VitaminWater because, well, VitaminWater is just delicious and you should drink it whenever the opportunity presents itself.

3. **Be fruity**. Head out to pick local produce—peaches, berries, or apples—or if you'd rather not get your hands dirty, head to the farmers' market and stock up on local cherries, plums, and pears, and then eat them together.

4. **Get a Groupon**. Recently on Groupon and Living Social, I've seen deals for an acrobatic ball ride, a water bike rental, a DIY pottery experience, and an ice cream–making course. All fun daytime date ideas. And all things you've probably never done before.

5. **Have an indoor picnic**. Send the kids off to Grandma's, and then lay a blanket on the living room floor and have an indoor picnic with things like bread, cheese, and chocolate-covered strawberries. (And, hey . . . the blanket is out on the floor . . . and the kids are at Grandma's, so . . .)

6. **Head to the cheap seats**. There's nothing like the view from the cheap seats (or so they say). Head to the ballpark and

splurge on five-dollar bleacher tickets, hot dogs, and even a pair of foam fingers. If you really want to make your hubby fall in love with you all over again, lean over and kiss him passionately every time your team scores a run.

7. **Get artsy.** My friend Kaimey and her husband actually signed up for a mini art class where they went to an art studio and an instructor helped them paint pictures together. Or, if you're feeling very adventurous, just head to the art store and pick up some canvases and paint and start creating.

8. **Kickbox.** Head to the gym—or if you're not a member, sign up for a free trial—and take a fun class together, like kickboxing or water aerobics.

9. **Sightsee your city.** Pretend you are tourists (which means it's totally acceptable to wear your fanny pack) and head to the local tourist attractions. Visit a monument. Tour city hall. Hold hands while you hike a historical trail.

10. **Wash your cars together.** Water, suds, your husband in his bathing suit. Enough said.

Reinventing Bedtime

Even after all this effort, there will still be times when you just can't find—or afford—a babysitter. But I have found a loophole: bedtime. Yes, that's right. There is absolutely nothing—well, nothing except your mommy exhaustion—standing in the way of you getting all lovey-dovey romantic after the kids go to bed. Try one of these fun "dates" that you can do from the comfort of your home after the little romance-stoppers are in zzz-land. (Bonus tip: A friend of mine told me that every Friday night, she moves her clocks up an hour and tricks her kids into an earlier bedtime so she and her husband can have an extra hour for "date night" at home. Genius parenting at its best.)

The Christian Mama's Guide to Parenting a Toddler

Ten Romantic "Dates" You Can Do from
Home (After the Kids Are Asleep)

1. **Plan a totally unaffordable vacation.** Snuggle up on the coach and plan that super-romantic vacation to Italy or Scotland or Thailand that you've always dreamed of. Who cares if you'll be able to afford to go, well, never? The planning is half the fun.

2. **Cook dinner together.** I know you can wait until eight o'clock for dinner—you used to do it all the time. So, grab a snack and feed the kids PB&J, and then cook a romantic dinner for two. Yes, leftover spaghetti totally counts, as long as you light candles and play footsies under the table while you eat.

3. **Play twenty questions.** Write down twenty things you want to know about your hubby—and have him do the same. Take turns asking and answering.

4. **Do karaoke.** You are not going to catch me singing at the mike in any karaoke bar—mostly because I'd probably get booed off the stage. But at home? In front of my hubby? Well, watch out, Kelly Clarkson. There's a new pop diva in town.

5. **Have a cookie-baking contest.** See who can come up with the most ooey-gooey delicious flavor. You'll probably need to taste several to be sure which one is best.

6. **Play poker.** Instead of betting money, bet back massage minutes.

7. **Swap movies.** Agree to watch any movie he chooses—even if it's some cheesy adventure-packed dynamo-boy movie, as long as he agrees to watch whatever sweet, romantic Lifetime special you're dying to watch the next night.

8. **Go outside.** You know that patio or yard you rarely use for anything besides playing in the sand table? Put it to good use. Steep some mugs of herbal tea, head outside, and plant yourself on your hubby's lap.

9. **Watch the game.** Embrace *Monday Night Football* (or Tuesday night rugby or whatever) by making it a romantic event. Make chips and dip, put on your team's colors, and watch together.

Just warn your husband that he can't get annoyed if you ask him who scored the last run during the game.

10. **Have sex**. Girl, I'm disappointed in you. You should've thought of this one on your own. See that guy sitting over there on the couch? The one looking at you with that cute come-hither grin? Go jump the man. Just don't wake up the kids.

Reinventing Your Sex Life

Sex. It was a whole lot of fun when you were first married, wasn't it? Way back when back massages made you want to do something more than just fall asleep and when a stolen glance across the room meant "let's go to *bed*" and not "let's go to bed." But now? It's mainly about trying to figure out how to fit it in between bedtime (theirs) and konk-out time (yours) while wondering if you really want someone else handling your breasts when you just finally got them back to yourself after weaning.

I'm guessing there was a time in your marriage when you saw your husband with his shirt off and didn't immediately assume someone had peed on him. A time when you actually had time to shave your legs at least once a week. A time when having sex rated higher on your list of to-dos than changing the liner in the Diaper Genie.

You can get back to that place! Sex with kids doesn't have to be ho-hum. And while I certainly don't want to even attempt to reinvent sex—I think God got that one right the first time—your sex life could probably use some spicing up. That or a complete overhaul. And now that your kid is big enough to do big-kid things, like sleep through the night and stay in bed until 7:00 a.m., it's the perfect time to reinvent your sex life. Here are my best tips.

Ten Fun Tips to Bring Back Your Honeymoon Period
1. **Challenge yourself**. Have you seen the book *Sexperiment* by pastor Ed Young? This pastor (yes, he's bona fide clergy!)

challenges married couples to have sex every day for seven days. Every single day! Mention this to your husband—and, well, I'm guessing he'll be making an Amazon purchase tonight. It is, after all, pastor's orders.

2. **Make sex a game**. I'm not telling you to tease your husband (not much, at least) but I don't see any reason why sex can't be fun. Play a game of (strip) UNO or (naked) Twister.

3. **Make a sex date**. Mommy comic Debi Gutierrez challenges wives to implement Woo Hoo Thursdays, guaranteeing their husbands a little, um, woo-hoo time every Thursday night. It not only gives him something to look forward to all day— heck, all week—but it also makes it übercertain that you'll put sex on your calendar at least once every seven days.

4. **Make out like newlyweds**. Who cares if people scream at you to get a room. You can just scream back that you already have one, *thankyouverymuch*. And it's stocked full of talking Yo Gabba Gabba toys and monkey stuffed animals.

5. **Surprise your husband**. Go out of your way every once in a while to do something supersweet (and maybe a tad bit sexy) for your husband. Make chocolate-covered strawberries as an after-bedtime treat, or wear a new pair of sexy undies under your skirt to dinner.

6. **Baby-proof your bedroom**. Considering the fact that there is nothing less sexy than diapers and wipes (well, except for maybe changing diapers with said wipes), it's time to give baby stuff the heave-ho from your master bedroom. Good-bye, singing and flashing animal train; hello, romantic candles.

7. **Save nighttime for sleep (at least sometimes)**. There is absolutely nothing that beats the feeling of a good, long, and uninterrupted night's sleep. So if you're too tired for anything but sleep at night, try mixing it up and having sex in the morning before your kid wakes up. And if that's a fantasy that simply will never happen with your early-bird toddler, then you might have to get really creative. Naptime nooner anyone?

8. **Pamper yourself.** Get in the mood by taking a warm bubble bath or going to get a mani-pedi.

9. **Go on a second (or tenth) honeymoon.** Schedule some honeymooning time away overnight at a hotel. Or if you can't swing that, arrange to have a friend or grandma host a slumber party for your kids, and then turn your house into a regular Hotel Romántico.

10. **Switch up the location.** I'm not afraid to be labeled as boring: I like sex in a bed. I like clean sheets and pillows and being able to fall asleep in my husband's arms afterward. But since we're reinventing our inner sexy mamas, I figure we could all try to stretch ourselves a little. Which means if you want to have sex, say, in the living room or on the stairs, I say go for it.

Romance, Reinvented

Not to get all pseudo-inspirational on you, but your marriage is important. And while nothing—except pregnancy—makes me more nauseous than when people try to pass off sayings like "Love makes the world go round" as motivational, I also have to confess that there's a little truth in that romantic nugget. God considers your marriage the most important earthly relationship you have. Plus, the relationship you have with your husband sets the stage for how your kids view their future relationships and their kids view their future relationships. Sappy as it sounds, your love kind of does make the world go round.

I hope this little pep talk has inspired you to think big for your relationship. To reinvent your romance to make it better and bigger than you ever imagined it would be. You have the tools. I have the patent (or at least I like to think I do). Now all you need is a babysitter, some time, and your man. Oh, and you might want to go change your underwear—those granny panties just aren't going to cut it anymore.

SIXTEEN

Doing It All Over Again

Getting Prepped and Ready for Round 2 (or 3 or 4)

have no idea where you are in your life. You could be reading this when you're right in the crux of the up-all-night mayhem that comes from having a toddler—in which case you should probably bookmark this page and come back to it in a year or two when you'll certainly be thinking more clearly. But you could also be in that place where you're starting to think about, you know, doing it again. You may have fallen so completely head-over-heels in love with motherhood that there is no doubt that you want another one. And maybe a few more after that. And, whether you're actively trying or just thinking of getting pregnant again, there's a whole new level of calisthenics involved when you're juggling a baby or toddler on top of trying.

I got pregnant with my second, Kate, when Joey was just

eleven months old. And while it was really hard at times—I'm not sure I would recommend trying to deal with a one-year-old and morning sickness simultaneously—it's also kind of great to have two kids who are less than two years apart and have never really known life without each other. I love that.

I'm not going to even pretend to know anything about ideal baby spacing—that's a decision for you and your family—but once you do make the decision, I can help you along a little bit with the whole getting-pregnant-again thing. Here's what you need to know.

Getting Knocked Up

Even if you have been pregnant before and are quite aware of *how* babies are made, getting pregnant again is not as easy as just going to bed and waking up pregnant. And whether you struggled the first time or got pregnant in one try, there are always a lot of factors when it comes to getting pregnant. There's timing to consider. And stress. And sleep. And nutrition. And overall health. And a million other things that make getting pregnant much harder than expected.

I confess: I am one of those people who got pregnant just by looking at my husband. In fact, I got pregnant with my son while using, like, four types of birth control (okay, just one) and following the rhythm method. Several of my friends, on the other hand, spent several months, or even years, trying. Most of them eventually got pregnant, but I watched them go through the roller coaster of waiting and hoping each month, only to be disappointed. I know it wasn't easy.

I know a lot of women who went to great lengths to get pregnant. And I have some friends who struggled even more on their second pregnancies than on their first. Some used Clomid (a fertility drug), and others had in-vitro fertilization. One friend ended up adopting her babies after years of trying. So while I don't want to be a Debbie Downer right when you start dreaming about another baby, I want to point out that getting pregnant—even getting pregnant for the second time—isn't always easy—and it doesn't always go the way you expect.

So buckle your seat belt (you may want to get one of those that adjusts to fit your blossoming belly) and get ready for the ride. It's sure to be a long one, so pack your cooler with lemon-scented water and saltine crackers and let's go. It's time to get knocked up.

The Baby Bug

My first pregnancy was, er, we'll call it a surprise. It wasn't that I didn't want a baby; it's that I didn't *know* I wanted a baby. I was young and loved my career and wasn't quite ready for the mommy stage. In fact, for weeks after that big, fat positive test, I was sure that the agony of pregnancy wasn't going to be worth it. Of course, the instant I held the little guy, there was no looking back. I was in love.

As I already told you, I adored my son so much that right before he turned one, I got the baby bug. *Bad.* It came on all of a sudden. I was reading a magazine that labeled one-year-olds as toddlers, and I realized with a jolt that my baby wasn't really a *baby* anymore. He was a big boy! My baby was all grown up . . . and I wanted (*needed*) another one.

That's the thing about babies. You go through nine months of morning sickness, weight gain, bloating, and contractions—and as soon as you hold that baby in your arms, you forget every painful moment of your pregnancy. Babies are mind erasers. One baby giggle and every negative pregnancy-related memory is forgotten. But you already know that.

After my realization that my baby was a big boy, the baby bug wouldn't go away. I had it bad. I'd see a baby in the mall and I'd practically rip it out of his mother's arms just so I could get my baby fix. I cooed over baby clothes, cried at baby showers, and (*sigh*) coveted my sister-in-law's pregnancy. I remember walking through the diaper aisle at Target and seeing those packages of teeny-tiny Pampers Swaddlers diapers and telling my mom how depressed I was that I couldn't buy Swaddlers anymore. My baby had (sob!) graduated to Cruisers diapers. See? I had it bad!

My husband took some convincing. He *hadn't* forgotten the pregnancy (and he wasn't even the one who had to go through labor!). I reminded him that trying meant sex, something we hadn't done a lot of since the baby was born—and even that wasn't enough to persuade him. He wanted to make sure I would be able to handle another difficult pregnancy *while* taking care of my son. He also wanted to make sure I was healthy enough to carry another baby so soon. He had all sorts of concerns.

The truth? He had good reason to have reservations. But rational reservations are nothing compared to a woman with a bad case of the baby bug. I promised him it'd be okay. I promised I'd eat healthfully. I even promised I'd limit middle-of-the-night trips to get ice cream and pickles. I was willing to make a lot of concessions if it meant another baby. I'm sure it was my charming personality coupled with my ragged, worn-out appearance that did the trick—I convinced him.

Trying

For our first night of "trying," I made big romantic plans. I popped my husband's favorite dinner in the oven and bought a set of racy baby doll lingerie. I set the table with flowers and candles and put Norah Jones on the iPod. We tucked my son in bed early and giggled like newlyweds the entire night. It was—*ahem*—one of the best nights of our marriage. The next morning I woke up entangled in my husband's arms, and we "tried" again. May as well give it our best possible shot, right?

The next night, we tried again. Twice. And the next. And the next. And the next. We tried for a week straight. It was fun and romantic at first, but after a while (I can't believe I'm going to admit this!), I got tired of it. I would've done anything for a night of lounging on the couch in my grandmotherly flannel pj's watching *Law & Order* reruns.

I was burned out on trying, and it had only been a few days! The funny thing is that I think my husband was burned out too. Of course, he would never admit this, but he didn't put up too big of a fight when I suggested a night off. By the time I had my flannels on, he had made popcorn and was already thumbing through the channels.

My point? Trying can be fun and romantic and a real intimacy builder in your marriage, but it can also be exhausting. So if you're feeling burnt out, or are just needing a break, don't be afraid to tell your spouse. Chances are he's feeling the same way.

Tips for Trying:

1. Take it slow. I know; I already said this, but I'll say it again. There's no need to have sex four times a day—or even four times a week. In fact, I think I read in one of my fancy medical pregnancy guides that your chances of getting pregnant actually *increase* when you only have sex every other day.

2. Make it fun. Sex can suddenly start to feel like a job if you are only focusing on trying to get pregnant. Have fun! Wear sexy lingerie. Go on a date. Have sex in your living room—or your car. Be creative. I'm sure you'll figure something out.

3. Try not to stress about your fertile days. I remember looking at a fertility calendar when I was trying and suddenly feeling all sorts of pressure to perform. Even if you know your most fertile days, try to treat them like any other day.

4. Eat and sleep as though you're pregnant. Eat healthy, sleep a lot, the usual blah-blah-blah, but you're going to need all the energy you can to carry that baby, so you may as well get started now.

5. Exercise. Bonus points if you exercise *with* your spouse. Try

going on a walk together after dinner, or pop in a Tae Bo DVD and get moving. May as well get into shape now, 'cause if you're anything like me, you'll find pregnancy is the perfect excuse to avoid exercise at all cost.

6. Spend some time with your partner outside of trying. It's easy to get caught up in sex, sex, sex when you're trying, but make sure you spend some time just being together and not having sex. Go to the movies, trade massages, watch a favorite TV show, or play a board game.

Waiting, Waiting, Waiting . . .

The thing about pregnancy is that the symptoms don't show up right away. You don't wake up one morning and suddenly have a cute round belly, glowing cheeks, and great hair. Instead there's this long (okay, two- or three-week) period of time where you're stuck in limbo. You might be pregnant. You might not. And every little twinge in your belly or ache in your back will set your mind whirring with the possibility.

Honestly, I think there's just something about early pregnancy that messes with your mind. It's as if the moment you conceive, a chemical is released into your body that suddenly turns you into an irrational, mood-swinging mess. The worst part is that in those few weeks before you know you're pregnant, you have to pretend everything is normal while this crazy flood of hormones is surging through your body and making you, well, crazy.

Case in point: Me. I am not a patient person. I want to be. I pray for patience (and in turn, God gives me more opportunities to *learn* patience). But I hate to wait. So waiting to know if I was (or wasn't) pregnant drove me nuts.

I remember scouring the Internet to find out the absolute, tip-top, utmost, without-a-doubt earliest that a pregnancy test could come back positive. While I did find a few articles that said I could take a home pregnancy test as many as seven days before my period (music to my ears!), the general online consensus was that it's best to wait at least until the day your period should start. Really, the day your miss your period? Doesn't that kind of negate the point? Someone has *got* to invent a morning-after pregnancy test.

I'm sure there are (patient) women out there who wait until their period is due to take a test, but I am *not* one of those patient people. I bought a jumbo-sized pack of pregnancy tests at Costco an entire week before my period was due because the box said, "Results sooner than any other test." The package directions said that, if taken five days before a missed period, a woman who is actually pregnant has a 53 percent chance of getting a positive result. Those odds were good enough for me.

For some reason my husband (did I mention that he's practical?) didn't like those odds. He happens to be the most patient man on the planet and happens to think that spending nine whole dollars on a pregnancy test with 53 percent odds is a waste of money. He pointed out that I'd have a 98 percent chance of getting a positive result if I just waited five days.

Here's a helpful hint to any potential dads-to-be who are reading this: Saving nine bucks is not worth the pain and aggravation it will cause when you tell your wife that she can't take a pregnancy test. There's no explaining odds to a possibly-pregnant (read: emotional and hormonal) woman. And if your wife wants to waste one (or three) pregnancy tests by taking them early, let her. My husband learned that lesson rather quickly after the five-day-53-percent debacle and actually suggested I take a test three days before my period was due. I was happy to oblige. And, if you must know, it was negative.

I also took a test two days before my period was due (negative) and one day before my period was due (negative) and on the day my period was due (negative). The crazy thing is that I actually *was* pregnant with my daughter . . . but I didn't get a positive result on a home pregnancy test until two days after I missed my period.

So, technically, I guess everyone knows what they're talking about when they say to wait to take a test. But I'm not one for technicalities.

My husband (who *is* one for technicalities) has banned me from taking pregnancy tests in my next pregnancy. He said that I could just wait and find out the old-fashioned way (ie, waiting for weeks until you start showing to know for sure). Let's just say I accidentally forgot that rule one morning after he went to work.

. . . .

Time-Out for Mom

For When You're Praying for Another Baby

"But he said to me, 'My grace is sufficient for you, for my power is made perfect in weakness.'" (2 Corinthians 12:9)

Father God, Your grace is sufficient for me! And in this time that I am praying that You will choose to bless us with another beautiful life to add to our family, I also trust You and Your perfect will for our lives. Lord, it's so hard for me to be patient, but I know that You have a perfect plan and that it will be revealed in Your timing. I pray that You grant me peace and serenity as I wait to see Your will unfold. Amen.

. . . .

Signs of Pregnancy

While you are waiting to take that test, there's no reason to sit around eating bonbons when there's so much obsessing to do! Personally, I spent those two weeks obsessing over every little ache and pain. My boob hurt. I spent all day researching pregnancy and thinking about the possible pregnancy disaster that could have resulted in boob pain, until I realized that the underwire on my bra was just cutting into my side. I yawned. I translated that to pregnancy exhaustion, for sure. I felt sick. Must be morning sickness.

If you're in that obsessing (er, researching) stage, here's a list of pregnancy signs and symptoms for you to obsess over. Of course, you could have none of these and still be pregnant—or you could have all of them and not be. You'll notice that a lot of the early pregnancy signs are suspiciously similar to signs of PMS, which makes it kind of tricky to discern whether you're preggo, especially since the alternative is your period.

You Might Be Knocked Up IF . . .

1. You're having trouble staying awake through *Downton Abbey*.
2. Your boobs hurt.
3. You're exhausted. A trip to the grocery store to buy a carton of milk sounds about as difficult as running a marathon in your knee-high boots.
4. You're starving. You eat six doughnuts, four scrambled eggs, a handful of grapes, and a glass of orange juice for breakfast and still need a snack by 9 a.m.
5. You're nauseous. This usually starts a few weeks after you miss your period, but some (lucky) women start feeling queasy earlier.
6. You press sleep on your alarm clock an average of four times each morning.
7. You're bloated. This could be the result of the entire bag of potato chips you ate last night (see #4), but it also can be an early sign of pregnancy.
8. You can tell by sniffing the air that your neighbors ordered Chinese for dinner and your husband forgot to put on his deodorant.
9. You have to pee every twelve seconds or so. Something about the hormone rush of early pregnancy puts your bladder into hyperdrive.

10. You have an incessant urge to take pregnancy tests over and over . . . even if your period isn't due for days.

When Your Period Starts

Chances are you won't get pregnant the first month you start trying. It'd be nice, but it doesn't usually happen that way. Instead, most couples try for several months before they get a positive result. Several months! In fact, my doctor told me once that a year of trying is considered *normal*. A year may not seem like a long time, but to someone living in a constant maybe-pregnant state, that means a year living on a roller coaster.

When your period starts, it's easy to feel disappointed (okay, devastated). Rationally, you know that it's normal, but it's not easy to be rational when you are disappointed, upset, and you have your period to boot! It's okay to be disappointed. It's even okay to be upset. God's timing may not be your timing, but God's timing is omniscient (fancy church talk for all-knowing), and He knows everything you want and need. You'll get there, and in the meantime, your job is to trust Him. Tough job, huh?

It also wouldn't hurt to do a little something to cheer yourself up after yet another "not pregnant" result. Have what I affectionately call a "not-preggo party" and do something fun or eat something delicious that you could never do if you were pregnant. And enjoy every non-pregnant moment. Trust me: you'll miss these things during nine months of deprivation.

Things You Can Do When Your Period Lets
You Know You're Not Pregnant
1. Go out for sushi. Eat raw fish to your heart's content, and pile on the wasabi (without worrying about pregnancy heartburn).
2. Get your hair highlighted.
3. Sleep on your stomach.

4. Indulge in a venti triple-shot latte (*with* whip), and enjoy every caffeinated sip.

5. Stay up late. Watch a great movie and eat popcorn. If you were tired and pregnant, you'd never be able to make it through the opening credits.

6. Go on a long bike ride. Go horseback riding. Go to a theme park and ride every roller coaster.

7. Buy some sexy (non-maternity) lingerie and get ready to start trying again.

8. Have a turkey-and-brie sandwich.

9. Wear your favorite jeans to work. Dress code, whatever! You won't be wearing them for long, so enjoy while them you can.

That Big, Fat, Positive Test

Now for the good part: most likely, there will be a day that you actually pee on a stick (or a series of sticks one after another after another much to your husband's chagrin) and two blue lines appear. If you're anything like me, the first thing you'll do is shake the test as hard as you can just to make sure you aren't seeing things. Then you'll probably tear open another nine-dollar pregnancy test and pee on it, just to make sure the first one wasn't somehow flawed. After three or four such tests, you'll run screaming with the pee-soaked test(s) and leap into bed, where your husband is sleeping, and fling the still-dripping test in his face while he groggily tries to figure out why there's pee on his head.

Exciting, huh? And a bit shocking. Even if you were trying to get pregnant, the news that trying actually *worked* comes as quite a shock. I recommend spending a few minutes letting the reality of the fact soak in. I know you're just itching to start picking out nursery bedding, but give yourself a few days to bask in the news. It's big news. Okay, huge news. And it's okay to walk around town, chanting in a singsongy voice, "I'm having a baby! I'm having a baby!" 'Cause you are!

Telling Your Family

My decision to keep my pregnancy a secret "through the first trimester" lasted about as long as it took me to speed-dial my mom and excitedly blurt, "I'm not supposed to tell you yet, but you're never going to believe this . . . I'm pregnant!" I was never good at keeping secrets anyway. Within days (okay, hours) our entire family and most of our friends and acquaintances knew about our impending family addition.

I don't have any secret-keeping capacity at all, so the entire universe found out I was pregnant right away. On the other hand, many couples wait until they are through their first trimester to tell their families (which is fine, by the way, although your family members might not think so). My brother and sister-in-law waited until they were (gasp!) ten weeks along to tell me (and yes, I'm still a bit bitter).

If you are one of those people who does have the patience to wait and the mental fortitude (hormones and all), you may want to think of a special way to announce your pregnancy. Oftentimes the best ways are the ways that are sentimental or significant to you and your family. When I was pregnant with my daughter, my sister-in-law brought me a baby shower gift. Inside the bag were two matching outfits. I was a little confused (why did I need *two* identical outfits?), but suddenly the light went off on my head. She was pregnant too! One outfit was for my baby and one was for hers!

Another friend of mine planned a huge party to announce her pregnancy. When I arrived at her house, it seemed like any other dinner party. In reality, the whole place was baby-themed. We ate baby back ribs and baby corn salad for dinner and had mini éclairs for dessert. She covertly placed random baby items around the house for us to find—a baby bottle on the dish rack, a tiny T-shirt hanging on the coat rack, and little booties by the door. She even wore a T-shirt that said, "Baby on board." No one even noticed the theme for a while (and I admit, I was one of the last to catch on), but when we figured it out, the entire place erupted in cheers. What a fun way to announce a pregnancy!

Mommy of One Turns to Mommy of More

Naturally, once you get over the crazy, insane I'm-going-to-have-another-baby excitement, you're going to have to deal with the crazy, insane, I'm-going-to-have-another-baby terror. And then the crazy, insane, I'm-going-to-have-another-baby, why-did-I-think-this-was-a-good-idea anxiety. And eventually, after downing six Häagen-Dazs bars in one sitting, you'll finally reach a place of giddy acceptance. Because as I said, parenthood is a roller coaster. But it's a fun roller coaster that I want to ride again. And again. And again.

Epilogue

Treasuring Two

My youngest, Will, is a handful. Okay, that's an understatement. He's two handfuls on a good day, and on a bad, well, let's just say I need an Energizer bunny attention span just to keep up with him. And whether he's putting the Costco-sized box of granola bars into the toilet (seriously, where does he come up with these things?) or riding our sweet old golden retriever, Jack, like a pony, he definitely keeps me on my toes.

Just last week, I was visiting my mom while Will sat on the piano bench and banged on the keys. I turned my back to check on my other kids—I swear, it took less than a minute—and when I turned around, Will was no longer sitting on the bench, but was now standing on *top* of the piano. Because that's safe.

I admit that there are days—many days—I am tempted to wish away these years. To wish him older. To wish I could trust him to go up the stairs by himself or not to eat rocks at the playground. Days when I wish I could sit down with my Bible and a cup of coffee without having to get up every twelve seconds to deal with my toddler who likes to get into anything and everything.

But I refuse to wish away time.

Because I know just how fast it can fly.

Just last year, my oldest son, Joey, started kindergarten. And as

I sent my baby out into the big, wide world—something I'll talk much more about in my next book, which is aptly named *The Christian Mama's Guide to the Grade School Years*—treasured moments from his baby and toddler years flashed through my mind. I remembered the day he was born—tiny, dependent, and just about perfect. I remembered the day he took his first steps. The day he said, "Mama" for the first time. And the day he climbed onto the dining room table and swung on the chandelier. And these treasured moments melded together to became treasured reflections on all the ways God had used motherhood to grow me.

I know that my other kids—my precious Kate and exuberant Will—will too soon follow Joey out into the big, wide world. And while I know that my days as a mom will never be done—and that even in grade school and beyond, those treasured moments will continue to come—I also know that each step forward also means a step away from me.

A step toward independence.

A step into the big, wide world.

And this is a good thing—we want our kids to learn and grow and to become the adults God created them to be. But not too quickly. And not without plenty of sweet toddler hugs and precious toddler smiles along the way.

And so, I'm choosing to treasure two. And three. And each and every moment I have when my kids are young and still need me to make sure they won't fall from the top of the entertainment center or eat that worm that mysteriously looks like a Froot Loop on the kitchen floor. And I pray that when the time comes for me to let go—to let my kids take those first independent steps—I'll have given them the tools they need to fly. Bravely and confidently. But with one eye looking back toward home so they can see that I'm cheering them on as they go.

About the Author

Erin MacPherson is a mom of three who wants to come beside her readers not only as a confidante and Christian sister, but also as a friend who understands what it's like to juggle kids, life, and a much-too-messy house. When she discovered she was pregnant she decided to write about it—but then kept writing. A former staff writer and editor for Nickelodeon, Erin now entertains parents on her personal blog, www.christianmamasguide.com, as well as through her staff writing job with WeAreTeachers.com, freelance magazine articles, devotionals and speaking. Erin, her assistant principal husband Cameron, and her kids Joey (7), Kate (5), and Will (1) live in Austin, Texas.

To my Christian mama friends:

Congrats on surviving the toddler years! I'm so glad we were able to take this journey together and I pray that your transition is full of tender and sweet moments.

I would love to hear more about you—and of course, your child. Please drop by my website at www.christianmamasguide.com or e-mail me at erin@christianmamasguide.com. I can't wait to get to know you better!

Blessings,
Erin

Index